LET'S GO TO GABON, CAMEROON, AND NAMIBIA

TERRY LISTER

WORDWORLD
PUBLISHING

COPYRIGHT

Copyright 2023@ Terry Lister
All rights reserved. No part of this publication may be reproduced, stored in a retrieval system, or transmitted, in any form or in any means- by electronic, mechanical, photocopying, recording or otherwise- without prior written permission.

Contents

1. Travel Quote v
2. Introduction vii
3. Chapter 1 11
4. Chapter 2 31
5. Chapter 3 55
6. Chapter 4 83
7. Chapter 5 103
8. Chapter 6 119
9. Chapter 7 135
10. Chapter 8 157
11. Conclusion 169
12. About the Author 171
13. Review Request 173
14. A New Day Dawns 175
15. Travels In Senegal, The Land of Peace and Purpose 179
16. The Gambia, The Smiling Coast 183
17. Peace, Joy and Love: Christmas Across Africa 187

Travel Quote:

To travel is to discover that everyone is wrong about other countries.
~Aldous Huxley, 1894-1963, British Philosopher~

INTRODUCTION

After two very interesting and enjoyable trips into West Africa, I was ready to move a little further south. As I considered where l would go, the usual consideration of civil disturbance was prominent in my decision-making. As a result, I had to bypass a few countries that, at another time, I might gladly visit.

After considerable thought, I decided to visit Gabon, Cameroon, Equatorial Guinea, and Namibia as I figured these to be an interesting mix. There are similarities in that all have beautiful forests (though in the case of Namibia the forest is replaced by desert), and all have an Atlantic coastline; however, in the case of Namibia, the weather conditions are such that one simply cannot swim in the freezing waters. Whilst they all have National Parks with wild animals, Namibia and Gabon only attract tourists to see the wildlife that exists. There are other differences as well, which can be traced back to how colonialism impacted each country.

My intent was to see how the people in each country lived under the circumstances that found facing them. I was pleased to learn that post-independence, none of these countries had suffered civil war. Despite this, there was the issue of perceived one-party rule in at least two of the countries. This concerned me. In addition, the corruption ranking some of these countries had could hinder future development.

Sadly, the continued health challenge brought about by HIV-Aids still impacts these countries to varying degrees. In at least one of the nations, this results in lower life expectancy. However, I was pleased to learn of higher school attendance and resultant strong literacy rates in these countries. Free schooling at the primary level is also a huge positive.

The economic standing of each of these countries was relatively strong with none being considered third world or breadbasket countries; however, ensuring that each person has a job, a home and in turn, a satisfactory standard of living remains an elusive goal. Whilst the goods and services that provide a higher standard of living are present in these jurisdictions, the task facing the governments is how to get sufficient income to every family. How to actually do this in a way that is fair to all sectors of the community may be challenging. Housing and equitable land distribution must be a great concern to some of the governments.

To be forewarned is to be forearmed. Hence, armed with this information, I set off for my adventure knowing I would see many enjoyable sights, but l would also be knowing I'd also be bothered by some of the practices I would encounter.

(Equatorial Guinea)
Cameroon
0 100 km
0 75 mi
Atlantic Ocean
2°
Bitam
Minvoul
Oyem
Equatorial Guinea
Woleu R.
Okano R.
Mékambo
Cocobeach
Médouneu
Mitzic
Ivindo R.
Como R.
Makokou
Libreville
Ntoum
Lara
Ovan
Gabon R.
Kango
Foulenzem
Ogooué R.
Booué
Equator
0°
Ndjolé
Bifoum
Port Gentil
Gabon
Okandja
Aboumi
Ogooué R.
Lambaréné
Lac Onangué
Iboundji
Lastoursville
Koula-Moutou
Akiéni
Fougamou
Ngounié R.
Lagune Nkomi
Mimongo
Léconi
Omboué
Mandji
Franceville
Bongoville
Lagune Ngobé
Mouila
Mbigou
2°
Guietsou
Lébamba
Boumango
Lagune Ndogo
Moabi
Sette Cama
Tchibanga
Nyanga R.
Mayumba
Lagune Banio
Moulèngui Binza
Congo
Ndindi
4°
10°
©1997 MAGELLAN Geographix℠
(805) 685-3100 www.maps.com
12°
Angola
Zaire
14°

I was back on the road again! In uniform and roaring out of the blocks. I flew from Bermuda to JFK and then on to Charles de Gaulle (CDG) airport in Paris. When I took my first trip to Africa last fall, I went through this same airport but apparently had missed something. This time when I arrived at 5:30 AM, I found my way to a free passenger lounge. For those of you who have used it, you know how nice it is. For those who have not, when you're routed through CDG do use it. It's very attractive, sporting a room with nice couches to sleep on and another with chairs, couches, and a large screen TV. There are two places to buy food, one self-service and the other with wait staff. It was a nice place to wait out my 1:35 PM departure.

I finally arrived at Libreville, Gabon on Wednesday at 7:30 PM, having left Bermuda at 8:30 AM the previous day. It was another long journey but the excitement of getting to my destination made me forget any complaints I had in transit. I was situated in a very convenient location in a quality hotel where generally I found the staff both caring and accommodating. I was happy to have a tasty buffet breakfast each morning.

The *following* day, I engaged in the usual exercise of sorting out money and SIM cards, then I was off to the Musee des Arts et Tradition. they didn't allow pictures, so once again, I must tell the story without visual aids.

The museum is located at 51 Ave Augustin near the oceanside in a small building. There are displays of masks from the different tribes which are well-designed - and well preserved. In fact, the collection of masks and relics is simply amazing. I had a very knowledgeable English-speaking guide who gave the history and current use of each mask and relic. He was so thorough in his storytelling that my visit to this small museum lasted more than two hours. In addition to an outstanding collection of masks and relics, there was also a selection of musical instruments used in Gabon by tribesmen both in the past and current day.

Overall, was a wonderful start to my trip. Having first-hand exposure to the customs of the various tribes was very intriguing. I was now able to get a proper rest, as I had nothing else planned for the day.

I went to the Raponda Walker Arboretum in Mondah Forest the next day. Some years back, the last president of Gabon declared thirteen national parks. As a result, a significant percentage of the land is preserved forever. Overall, it is estimated that over 80% of the country's land mass is forest.

Mondah Forest, six miles north of the city, is one such park. Within the park is the reserve, which is named after a Gabonese priest, author, and naturalist. The arboretum has an amazing biodiversity which is definitely worth seeing. My initial plan had been to see, but some wildlife in Gabon simultaneously being educated of the various tree properties within the forest couldn't be a bad thing!

There was extensive lush vegetation and breathtaking trees. I had a guide who walked me through one of the trails and explained the properties of those trees that had signature plates. I'll share some of the ways in which the ancestors and some modern families put these trees to use with you.

The first tree was named *ozouga* (Sacoglottis gabonensis), the bitter bark tree. The fruit of this tree is enjoyed by elephants during the fruit season, which is from August to November, and it grows up to 23 m tall.

Ozouga tree

The second tree we examined was the *andok* (Iringia gabonensis), a wild mango tree. Its fruit is good for both man and animals and has a sweet taste, similar to mangoes we're accustomed to in the western world. People use it to make a soup called Odika. It's eaten with chicken or fish, its sweetness added to the savory flavouring.

The next tree was the *ozigo* (Dacryodes buttneri), which bore edible fruits that are good for both man and animals as well. In particular, by chimpanzees and gorillas who cannot get enough of it. People usually boil it. In the past, this tree was used to make cabinets; however, the government has banned the commercial use of this tree.

The fourth tree, called the *okoume* tree (Aucoumea klaineana), is a large timber producing tree and is extremely important for its variety of uses. The tree bark can be used to make paper for window blinds. It can also be used in furniture production. Its sap has several uses including in the Bitimi ceremony, celebrated by certain tribes and can also be used for perfume. Additionally, the sap can be used to start a fire and can also be consumed as purified water. Finally, the bark can be crushed and used as a powder.

As we walked through the forest we came upon the next tree,

known as the *azobe*, (Lophira alata), red ironwood tree. This tree has a very hard wood. As a result, it is often used as an underlay when new roads are being built. Its fruit is a small berry eaten by the animals.

The guide then told me about a tree called *initia*. Accordingly, this tree is deemed to have malaria solving properties. Looking closely at one, I could see carvings which had been taken from it. The pieces carved off are boiled and put in the ill person's mouth as part of the treatment to kill malaria.

The seventh tree was named *sorro*. Its red sap is used as an antiseptic by mixing it with water. This mixture heals wounds. My guide also told me that black panthers use this tree to make their claws stronger. Imagine! I should point out that the black panthers of Gabon are really leopards who have a skin pigmentation issue which results in their black colouring.

The *okala* (Xylopia aethiopica) is another very strong tree. Its bark is used to cover the walls of homes in the villages. Its presence is helpful in keeping snakes away, as they find it difficult to get inside huts which are covered with this material.

Next, the guide gave me a fern, which had a lovely smell. It could easily have been a popular perfume or soap, but it's used for medical treatments.

The last tree we studied during our time in the forest was the *olonvogo*. This tree had spikes which are broken off and used in a formula to help new mothers who cannot make enough milk for their babies.

For me, this three-hour morning walk in the woods was a wonderful learning experience, which effectively brought those tales we grew up with about how grandma and her grandma used to go outside and find plants and herbs to cure all ailments to life. Here, one was able to see tall trees in the forest and, if you didn't consider them having these various properties, it would go right by you!

The Mondah forest

OVERNIGHT TO LOPE NATIONAL PARK

I left Libreville by train at 7:30 PM (it was scheduled to leave at 6:45 PM... should I have been worried?) I had a comfortable first-class seat. There was a food car at the back of the train with decent cuisine and movies were shown throughout the journey. My car was air conditioned and maintained a nice temperature.

This was my first train ride in Africa, as there were only two other trains that existed in the countries I visited during my first two trips—a freight train in Mauritania (which some daredevils ride for the excitement) and a passenger train in Darkar, Senegal (which was deemed to be quite unreliable, so I never considered riding on it). I should point out that I never had a train ride in Central or South America either, as there are very few.

The need for a train to allow people and goods to move across the country was recognised in Gabon in the 1890s, but construction wasn't started until the 1970s, and finally, the railway system was completed in stages by 1987. Even today the train carries far more freight than people. From end to end, the train covers a distance of almost 450 km. Originally built by the government, it was privatized in 1997 after only ten years.

Lope National Park is inland some 250 km from Libreville. The train journey should have been just under six hours if it ran on time.

Keyword: *if*.

As it turned out, we were having a lovely ride until around midnight when the train came to a dead halt. Someone said something about an elephant, so I got out and joined the other interested folks going to the front of the train. Sadly, a young elephant had been on the tracks and was killed, with half its body trapped under the front of the train. Passengers took pictures, and I have some very graphic photos, which don't make good viewing.

Eventually there were lights on the track as a caboose approached from the direction in which we were heading, bringing a team of men who proceeded to cut the animal into pieces. Once sufficiently free, the train was able to reverse off the elephant and in time, we moved forward.

The train had been scheduled to arrive in Lope at 1 AM, but didn't arrive until 7:30 AM, due to the accident. Interestingly, the passengers stayed calm throughout the ordeal. I never saw or heard or heard anyone complaining about how long it was taking. As it turned out, I was mistakenly impressed that the passengers could stay so calm in this difficult situation because the truth more likely was, the passengers only stayed calm because they were used to being late on this train. Of course, I didn't sleep during this period, so I was very tired when I got to the hotel. Having arrived at 7:30 AM, the hotel safari vehicle picked me up and took me to the hotel where I was given breakfast before going to bed until noon.

The first activity was a safari drive, which lasted from 4 PM to 6:30 PM. Lope National Park was the first reserve created by the government in 1947. It was on the list of thirteen national parks declared in 2003 by President Omar Bongo, and in 2007 it was made a UNESCO site. The train coming to Lope in the 1980s made the park accessible to people.

Among the many animals that live in this National Park are forest elephants, gorillas, chimpanzees, forest buffalo, black colobus monkeys, rhinoceros, and leopards. This is a good variety of animals. I'd be thoroughly pleased should I succeed in seeing most of them and was excited about this game drive; but that excitement turned to disappointment as we saw only six rhinos and two elephants. Nor did I see many birds.

Having said this, the two elephants were at separate locations. This would indicate that they were males, as these elephants travel in small groups of three to five—a mother and female offspring and sisters. As soon as the males can take care of themselves, they are sent away. Our safari drive saw a mature elephant and a young male moving about on their own. The only time the males mix with the females is during mating season.

This solitary pattern makes poaching easy, and this national park has suffered much poaching over the years. Also making poaching easier is the fact that the forest elephant is the smallest of the elephant family. Even now there is no indication that this deadly problem has been effectively dealt with. Over the past forty years, the forest elephant population has fallen by 80%. Interestingly, the estimated 95,000 forest elephants in Gabon represent 50% of the total population in Africa.

Forest elephant

SECOND DAY AT LOPE

The second day started at 7:30 AM with a climb of Mount Brazza. Reaching the top (500 m), one can get a very good view of the Ogooue river, which winds its way from east to west through the central part of the country and the landscape of the forest area. The climb took an hour on a gravel-like surface, and when we reached the top, we rested. I felt a bit of pain in my legs which was just a reminder that the biological clock says sixty-three not thirty-six.

LET'S GO TO GABON, CAMEROON, AND NAMIBIA 17

Mt. Brazza

View of the Ogooue River

At the very top there were solar panels—yup, even there in Gabon, an oil producing nation! The guide was very helpful in providing information about the area, which we surveyed from our lofty positions. We then trekked back down at a brisk pace and the views were simply marvelous.

The Lope village was bigger than I expected. It had a preschool for the families living there, and children transported elsewhere once they finished. There was also a small museum which I didn't get the chance to visit, as well as a few local restaurants, and at least three grocery stores were stationed in the area.

And, as one would expect, there were several bars.

There was an expensive hotel and a couple of cheap sleeps. My hotel was in between the two pricing levels, though still quite expensive.

I went on another safari drive at 4 PM, and this one started off great. We saw approximately twenty rhinos at the same spot in comparison to the we'd seen six the day before. After driving some more, we spotted about twenty-five forest buffaloes drinking. Forest buffaloes live in Central and Western Africa feeding off the Savannah grasses. They're the smallest of the buffalo family and tend to live in tiny herds of less than thirty animals. The herd I saw was large for this animal.

This was getting exciting.

Forest buffaloes

Later we saw four black colobus monkeys. These Central African monkeys live in small groups with one male, several females, and their offspring. Often, when spotting five or six swinging from tree to tree, this is one family. These monkeys can only be found in the forests of Equatorial Guinea, Cameroon, the Congo, and Gabon.

We saw more birds than the day before, and then there was nothing. For the next hour, the only things we saw were trees and tall grass! The biggest disappointment was that we didn't see mandrills. These beautiful monkeys are found in very few places in the wild, but Lope National Park is said to be the place where they can be found in greatest numbers, but, to be fair, looking at a map one can see that Lope is a large National Park so the area that I was touring in may have been quite a distance away from the closest mandrill. At 4,910 sq. km, Lope is the second largest park in Gabon.

View from Mt Brazza, Lope National Park

FRANCEVILLE AND THE POUBARA FALLS

After two days at Lope, I was supposed to leave by train at 1:40 AM, but the train didn't arrive until 4 AM. Why? The answer is still unknown. A memo may have been sent, but I didn't get to read it! Once the train arrived, I had to sit in the second-class (because I had a second-class ticket), and boy, what a mistake. The journey to Lope had seen a comfortable temperature in the first-class section. All had been quiet and orderly. Now in second-class, post-4 AM, there were young men walking the aisles, talking at the top of their lungs, and others were playing loud music.

The train ride covered roughly 150 miles and I was scheduled to arrive in Franceville, Gabon's third largest city, at 6:30 AM, with a full day of activities ahead. Instead, arrival was well past 10 AM. Sadly, no one explained why the train was late.

I was received by the man who was to run my two days of tours. He drove through the city and took me to a small hotel he seemed to own (or at least had a financial interest in). I took a couple of hours to try and recover from the previous night's experience, then had a large lunch, which consisted of a salad large enough for the two of us, rice and fish filets. Now, it's not my intention to offend any die-hard Bermuda fish lovers, but this was the best fish I've tasted in my life! I don't know what type of fish it was, though—most likely, a lake fish.

There was also a language barrier to contend with. My two-day tour guide spoke almost no English. This was one of those occasions where my inability/unwillingness to learn the local language left me severely restricted in terms of being able to respond to greetings.

Off to Poubara Falls and Suspension Bridge.

While driving, we passed a large billboard advertising a World Cup match actually played in November—there couldn't be much demand for that billboard, and I noted that the admission qualifier between Gabon and Mali was 500 cfa, which is less than a dollar! Imagine... Maybe that said something about the Gabon team, and when I raised it with my guide, he shook his head and said, "Gabon team is bad." At that point, Gabon was ranking around 120 in the FIFA men's football rankings. Like Bermuda, Gabon has never qualified for the World Cup.

The falls were about two hours away from the city. Driving along, I was enchanted by the beautiful landscape of rolling hills and Savannah grass until we entered the forest. Gabon has been an oil rich country since the 1930s, so (by and large) the roads are in very good condition; however, about twenty miles from the Falls, having turned off the main road, the quality fell away, and potholes ruled. The guide explained that a company had been given the contract to redo the road. Assurances had been given about payment, but halfway into the job they'd stopped, which resulted in the work eventually stopping as well.

As we neared the falls, we saw locked fencing behind which was all the equipment one would need to do this type of work. The guide explained that because they hadn't been paid, the company went bankrupt and there all its assets.

When we reached the falls, we saw the hydroelectric plant which had been built by the Chinese and has powered by the falls since 2013. To see the falls, one must cross over a suspension bridge. This bridge is made of liana vines. I experienced this in Labe, Guinea Conakry; however, this one, initially built in 1915, was a bigger, sturdier bridge and crossing it was easy. Despite this, I'm sure on windy days there are some folks who would prefer to stay on whichever side they're on.

Crossing the liana vine swing bridge

Once across the suspension bridge we walked to the falls along a rough pathway. The closer we got, water falling over the rocks sprayed us. I'd seen pictures of the falls—that's what drew me out there—but when I saw them in real life, I was disappointed. Unfortunately, they couldn't compare to any I'd previously seen in Africa and certainly not to those I visited during my stay in Labe last year.

Poubara Falls

After being there for a while, it started to rain so we quickly walked to the rapids which lead to another waterfall. To my disappointment, it wasn't accessible, and I hid my displeasure during the long drive back to the hotel. The only thing I wanted at that point was a bath, dinner, and bed.

It was approximately 6 PM when we arrived at the hotel. I got my bath and was told dinner would be ready at 8:30 PM, but it was actually served at 9:15 PM—chicken covered in salt and barely edible.

No happy ending to that day!

LECONI NATIONAL PARK

After the disappointment at Lope National Park, I moderated my expectations for Leconi National Park. This is one of the lesser-known and less-visited parks. The small town of 7,000 people, located on the banks of the River Leconi, is a two-hour drive northeast of Franceville and, once off the main road, there is a further hour-drive to the park gates.

Since it was so far away, the guide insisted we leave at 6 AM. Not being a morning person, this wasn't music to my ears, but I was ready—only to watch him poke around and do a whole lot of nothing for over an hour. We didn't leave until after 7 AM...

Along the way, I got to see the Gabon countryside once more, very beautiful and hardly populated. The country has a small population of just under two million. It's the 218th most densely populated country in the world with over 35% living in Libreville alone. The villages have been steadily abandoned by young people since independence, with the rural population being only 12% of the current population. One of the more serious results is that Gabon imports much of its food supplies. Even trying to find fruit in the markets is a challenge. Having so much open land, action must be taken to address this. Failure to act could lead to the country's inability to supply the basic foods needed to sustain the local population.

Once we entered the park the first difference was that we were driven around in a small but powerful jeep, unlike the usual safari vehicles. We then went on our game drive. To my delight, we saw large numbers of oryx, impala, and a few swift gazelles. The gazelles sprinted away when spotted, not to be seen again. Savannah grass covered the ground, and without any forest nearby, spotting the wildlife was much easier. Additionally, the oryx gathered in large herds. Occasionally one or two could be seen away from a herd but I assumed these were under punishment of some sort!

A herd of impalas

A herd of oryx

After experiencing the game park, we drove to the town of Leconi to see the Leconi Canyons. What a sight! There were three Canyons named after their colour: red, white, and green. The prettiest of the three is the Canyon Rouge. We went to the red canyon, which actually has twin Canyons, male and female. The male is the larger one. Now, I've been to the marvellous Grand Canyon and, yes, it is grand, but to be honest, these are *another* kind of special.

Leconi Canyons, 1

Leconi Canyons, 2

Leconi Canyons, 3

Looking at the map, you'll see how close Leconi is to the Republic of the Congo border. I'd gone deep into Gabon on this short one-week trip.

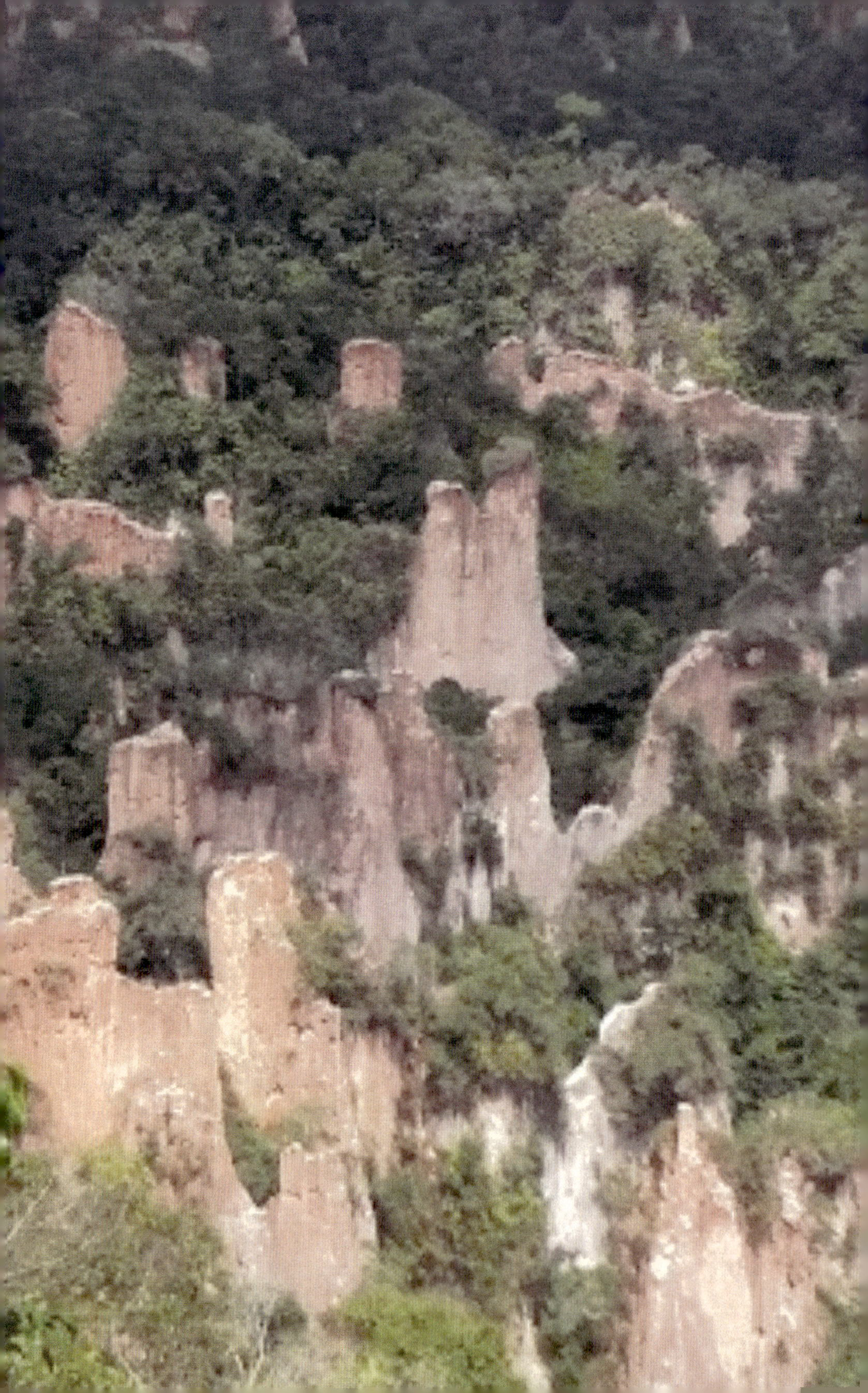

After having a fairly eventful day, it was time to head back to the hotel in Franceville and relax for a while before returning to Libreville by overnight train.

LIBREVILLE

I returned to Libreville, arriving at the train station at 8 PM. Of all the rides I'd had thus far on this train, this one seemed to have the most passengers. This didn't stop me from getting a lot of sleep, however, and I was out by midnight. Upon leaving the train station, I took a taxi to the hotel I'd stayed at before going on safari. They'd kindly secured my bag while I was away.

Upon reaching the hotel at 9 AM, the previously very nice lady at the front desk refused to allow me to have a room before noon. My arguments and pleas fell on deaf ears.

"It's not up to me. It's the rules," was her only response.

Unable to persuade her, I finally gave up, went to the guest bathroom, freshened up and headed for the dining room where I had breakfast at a snail's pace while reading my trip notes. It was so slow that when they came to get me at noon, I hadn't finished my breakfast—more than one way to skin a cat!

Since I'd be leaving for Cameroon at 4 AM, I took a slow day going to the ATM and visiting the Cathedral St. Marie. The original cathedral building isn't elegant at all. Instead, it's a significant historic monument, as it was the first mission founded by Christians in Gabon. Because of this, it's a simple church which includes a monastery as well as a modern church in front of it.

The old church

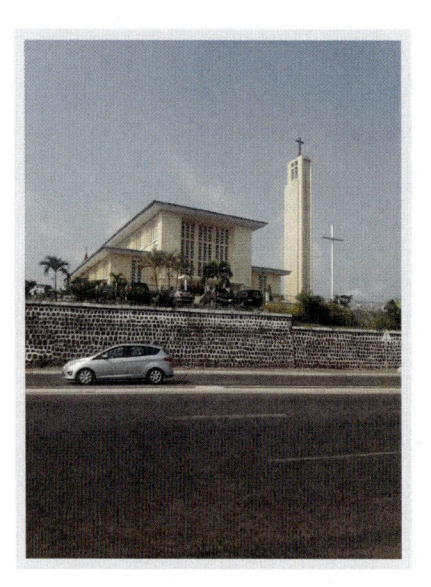

The new church

As I started back, I saw solar panels set out on the grounds of a government building. This makes a serous statement energy savings as Gabon gets its wealth from oil production.

Lastly, I bravely went for a haircut. This can be a nerve wrecking experience as prior to this I had four haircuts in Africa, two very good and two awful. In fact, the last haircut was in Accra from an English-speaking barber. After explaining what I wanted, he took the machine and ran it over my head, from back to front, as close as he could get it, leaving nothing!

Against this history, I entered the barbershop and engaged in a group conversation, which ended with the barber knowing exactly what I wanted. And I should add, I got a very nice cut. Lucky I found English speakers in the barbershop!

The time had come for me to go north to Cameroon. Thanks to my son, James, I had my visa in hand, so crossing the border should have been a smooth exercise. In this corner of the world, border crossings don't always go well (you may recall my experiences at the Senegal-Mauritania border). Knowing this, I had James get me a visa from the Cameroon embassy in London.

On this particular day, I was travelling by minivan, leaving at the ungodly hour of 4 AM. I was up at 2:45 AM, collected by pre-arranged taxi at 3 AM and delivered to the bus depot where I found about six people sleeping on the benches in the waiting area. My destination was a border town named Bitam, a mere 275 miles away.

We departed at 4:30 AM with about twelve passengers squeezed into the vehicle and as soon as we left the immediate area of the city we were on some rough roads (again, quite surprising in this oil rich country). For the next ninety minutes we were forced to drive slowly, and the pace picked up at daybreak. At approximately nine o'clock, we stopped, and I got breakfast, which consisted of a baguette filled with salad and ham—good dining.

As we returned to the journey, we started to run into a string of police checkpoints. At one of the first, there was a huge snake that had very recently been killed. This was evident due to the blood still flowing from it. I had a picture taken holding the snake, which I was made to understand was a Gabon viper. These snakes can grow up to seven feet and have the largest fangs of Gabonese snakes, two to three inches long.

Looks like I have dinner sorted out

The remainder of the trip was nothing more than an annoying routine of driving 20 km and then a police checkpoint followed by a second within a km. This was even more frustrating because the same people who'd been deemed to have improper paperwork were taken out of the van every time. They were given mini lectures and then invited to fix the situation by paying two mil (2,000 cfas or USD1.75). With this happening frequently, some got frustrated as the ticket cost for the journey was 14,000 cfas. So, seven hits of 2,000 cfas each doubles the price of the ticket. Terrible.

Later, I learned that many times the person knows his documents have been damaged and has gone to the appropriate government office only to be given a runaround that could result in receiving the new document many months later. Meanwhile, the person was subject to these crazy on the spot fines anytime he was on a public transit vehicle which was subject to being pulled aside. I went to the office six times. My documentation was examined twice, and I was subsequently sent back to the van. I was invited to pay 2,000 cfas on two occasions and politely declined before taking my documents and walking back to the van with a smile. On two occasions, when asked for the 2,000 cfas, I made partial payments of 1,000 and 1,500 cfas, respectively. Each time I was asked out of the van it was to have my yellow fever document examined (supposedly).

It was very late in the day when a police officer claimed I didn't have a visa. Now, think about this. The van had stopped no less than twenty times by that point. How could I have possibly gotten that far without a visa? Could it possibly have been a routine shakedown? I took my passport from the officer, turned to the correct page, and waited for him to send me back to the van, which he did with a look of disappointment. I guess he'd already decided what he was going to buy with my cash.

The continual stops turned the journey into an eleven-hour slog, and we arrived in Bitam at 3:30 PM, an average of twenty-five miles an hour. Feeling more than a bit tired, I looked around the village for only a short time before going to my hotel. I stayed there overnight, intent on crossing the border and going to the capital city of Cameroon the next day.

meroon
International boundary
Province boundary
National capital
Province capital
Railroad
Road
100 Kilometers
50
100 Miles
Mercator Projection
NIGER
NIGER
Lake Chad
NIGERIA
CHA
CENTRAL AFRICAN REPUBLIC
EQUATORIAL GUINEA
EQUATORIAL GUINEA
GABON
AND PRINCIPE
REPU
THE
EXTRÊME-NORD
NORD
ADAMAOUA
NORD-OUEST
SUD-OUEST
OUEST
CENTRE
EST
SUD
N'Djamena
Maiduguri
Potiskum
Kari
Bauchi
Gombe
Jos
Yola
Jalingo
Wukari
Garoua
Maroua
Mokolo
Kousseri
Waza
Mora
Fotokol
Makari
Guider
Figuil
Yagoua
Bongor
Kaélé
Poli
Tcholliré
Mbé
Touboro
Tignère
Ngaoundéré
Banyo
Tibati
Ngaoundal
Meiganga
Wum
Nkambe
Kumbo
Bamenda
Mamfe
Bafoussam
Dschang
Foumban
Bankim
Yoko
Garoua Boulaï
Bertoua
Batouri
Belabo
Nanga Eboko
Minta
Yaoundé
Mbalmayo
Abong Mbang
Yokadouma
Lomié
Ebolowa
Sangmélima
Djoum
Kribi
Campo
Ambam
Edéa
Eséka
Mfou
Akonolinga
Buea
Limbe
Kumba
Mundemba
Nkongsamba
Yabassi
Bafia
Monatélé
Ngoulémakong
Malabo
Luba
Bata
Ebebiyin
Bitam
Minvoul
Oyem
Mongomo
Souanké
Moloundou
Ouesso
Nola
Berbérati
Gamboula
Nddélé
Bouar
Baboua
Baïbokoum
Moundou
Pala
Léré
Lai
Fianga
Mubi
Bama
Bight of Biafra
Base 802577

Chapter 2
Yaounde and Bertoua, Cameroon

"I don't know where I am going, but I'm on my way."
~Unknown~

After gaining independence from France in 1960, there was a vote for reunification in 1961 that saw two separate countries come together under one flag. While many have deemed this to be a success there are others in the former British Cameroon who are now seeking the country be restored to its pre-reunification position. This issue has been argued over for several years; however, there is no sign that a solution is in sight.

Naturally, both French and English are the national languages. However, in reality, there are over 260 distinct linguistic groups. Life expectancy is low at under sixty years old. This is offset by low unemployment of only 4%. One of the factors contributing to the low unemployment rate is the high literacy rate which exists in the country. It's sad that 55% of the people live in poverty, while the average income is $1,600.

Cameroon has only had two presidents since 1960. The current 90-year-old president has been in power since 1982 and the governing party has been in office since independence. This situation has led to opposition to a one-party state from time to time and has resulted in allegations that corruption in the country is high.

That was the day I entered a new country, Cameroon. It would be the eleventh African nation I'd been to since October,2017. I left the hotel at 7:30 AM with my driver from the previous day. The front desk manager warned me that the police stops from the day before were mere child's play compared to what I'd encounter that day.

Not good news at all.

Before we reached the border, we passed through two police checkpoints. We then went to the Cameroon immigration office, and I got signed into Cameroon. We then drove twenty-four km to Kee Ossi, the Cameroon border point, without experiencing any problems. As it turned out, my hotel was quite a distance from the border.

It was approximately 9 AM when we arrived at the bus station. I bought my ticket for only 3,000 cfas, which is less than USD $6, but the SIM card sellers were unable to set up my phone even after putting the sim card in. Eventually everything except the internet was functional, and the three young men who'd been working on it gave up. Unfortunately, I couldn't find anyone to fix it until the following Sunday. So, once I was settled, I was forced to operate off the hotel's WIFI.

This was a part of my routine every time I crossed a border. First, I'd buy a SIM card, then I'd have to see if there was a plan. If there were plans, I had to figure out which was best for me—never an easy decision to make on the spot. Twice before, while in Ghana, I learnt the importance of having a plan after using up the money I'd put on my phone in one day instead of one week.

Hungry and with my business out of the way, I went looking for breakfast. To my dismay, I could only get a plate of cold spaghetti.

Yuck.

After forcing the food down my throat, the game of waiting for the bus to leave began, and at 11:40 AM, it finally departed. After being on the road for five minutes, we encountered our first police stop. We drove fifteen minutes more and the second stop presented. On this occasion, the officer took ten people off the bus after giving the busload a lecture about documentation. Finally, we were allowed to get back on the road at 1 PM. It was supposed to be a four-hour journey, but already it has been five hours since leaving the hotel in Bitam. We drove for a few more minutes and then made a stop. The bus loaded up with people and then simply sat there.

Well, it appeared as though I was on a local run—all 445 km of it!

We eventually set off and within minutes, we encountered a third police checkpoint. In my mind, this had become ridiculous—more time eaten up. I was getting uptight as I'd had my fair share of bus/train/van time in the last week. This pattern continued as the day drifted on. By 4 PM, nerves were frayed, and a verbal battle broke out between a male and female passenger. What they were fussing about, I'll never know but several of the women in close proximity joined in, coaching the female combatant! What a scene. Our day continued unbroken.

A building filled with beautiful caskets made by the local craftsmen

We finally reached Yaoundé at 8:45 PM, despite my hoping to be at the hotel by two o'clock in the afternoon! The man sitting beside me spoke English and said he'd secure a taxi for me. Another one of God's angels sent to assist me. I'd been warned that I shouldn't hang around the bus depot, as pickpockets roamed the place but here was the answer to the potential threat.

The taxi got me to the hotel at about 9:30 PM, and I immediately ran into a fuss. I had a confirmed two-night stay; however, my reservation, which had been made through *booking.com*, was at a very low price and the lady at the front desk refused to honour it! She wanted to double the rate! To be clear, I hadn't done any magic tricks to secure the rate I'd gotten. I'd simply used a trusted website and booked online.

Thankfully, the manager overrode her and accepted the rate, informing me that that their issue was with *booking.com*, not me. Apparently, the way the system works, when you book a room, it isn't confirmed until the hotel confirms it. So, the *hotel* had messed up. Well, we'd gotten that straight, but the lady continued giving me the evil eye. She was not a happy camper.

I went to the room and found that there was no running water in the bathroom. I reported this and they said their handy man would fix it right away. Not having eaten much since my spaghetti breakfast, I dropped my things and went in search of food. Not finding a restaurant anywhere nearby, I ended up getting odds and ends in a small grocery store nearby.

When I got back to the room there still was no water. It was 11 PM. Having left my last hotel at 7:30 in the morning, I was not eager for another fuss with the lady at the front desk but decided I should go back to her and politely ask for another room. While we were going back and forth the manager joins us just as she takes my money out of the drawer and tells me to take it and go! Can you imagine? I don't know anything about this city, but I was told to take my bags and go. Not that night, and the following one didn't look likely either. The resolution? A big tub of water put in my bathroom and a real plumber to come in the morning. Welcome to customer service!

After the previous night's drama, I was keen to be up and about the next morning. I took a taxi to the more central part of the city and started my own tour at the central market. Although still not a shopper, I've seen many markets, from Otavalo (near Quito, Ecuador), to the busyness of the Kusami market in Ghana, to the colour and life of the small market in St Louis in Senegal. That day, I was very surprised to find the central market was indoors in a series of two- and three-story buildings. It possessed neither the energy nor the colour one comes to expect from an African market.

Moving on from there, I went to Our Lady of Victories Catholic church. Built in 1952, it was undergoing renovations and would once more be a beauty. It can seat up to 500 people for a service. The interior is shaped like a cross, much like St Ann's church in Southampton, Bermuda. The steps leading up to the church must have been laid well over 150 years ago. There was a quaint prayer sanctuary beside the church that had drawings of Christ during the days leading up to the crucifixion.

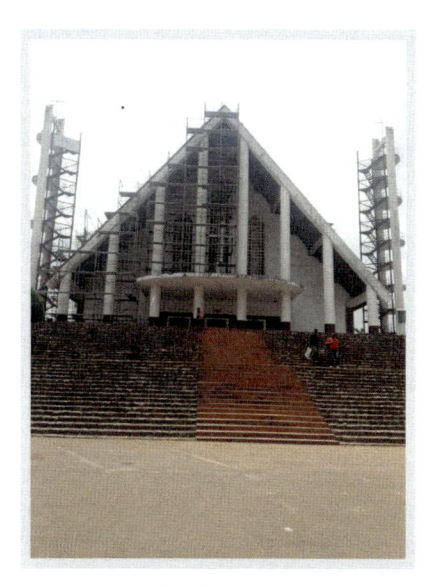

Our Lady of Victoria Catholic Church

I then went to the National Museum. When I approached to get a better view, I saw ladies and children in traditional costumes at the entrance. I asked what was going on and was told they would be part of a concert, which started at 3 PM. I was also given a flyer that certainly looked interesting enough, but it was after one o'clock, so I moved on—only to discover that the museum was closed. Just like in

Poubara Falls, disappointment washed over me. I really wanted to experience the museum, as it had a reputation for being one of the best in this part of Africa. The building itself was the presidential palace of the first president of Cameroon following independence, Ahmadou Ahidjo.

Not being able to enter the museum, I decided to spend the afternoon walking among the crowds shopping. I always find the goods for sale in the street quite interesting.

Outdoor beauty salon

As an added twist, I saw an outdoor hair salon. Several ladies were sitting on chairs in a line having their hair done. Another first for me. I'd never seen this before.

Early on Sunday morning, I took a taxi to the bus station to get a bus to Bertoua, which is in the southeastern area of the country.

Another long drive.

I left the city at around 10 AM and arrived in the town of Bertoua at approximately 6 PM. This bus made no rest or food stops. Thus far, I'd spent a significant percentage of my trip sitting on buses and other forms of transport. My lodging was a nice hotel; however, by the time I arrived and settled in, the kitchen had closed. As a result, I went to bed quite hungry.

The next morning, I traveled by bus some 80 km and visited the small town of Belabo. One of the more interesting things near this town is the Sanaga Yong Chimpanzee rescue centre. Established by an American veterinarian in 1998, this sanctuary is larger than the similar one I visited in Sierra Leone earlier in the year. While I was unable to visit, I was impressed by the work that has been going on in the forest for many years now. This work is so important as the number of chimpanzees in Africa is falling. The principal places where these animals can be found are the republic of the Congo, Gabon, and Cameroon. Many years ago, there were more than a million chimpanzees in Africa. Today, it's said that the total has been reduced to 150,000.

I was surprised by the mix of housing in the villages we passed along the way. There were villages with only wooden buildings, there were the Adobe-style buildings, houses built from clay brick, and lastly concrete block housing, much like those in Bermuda. As each style of house has a different cost attached, I was surprised to see this mix in small villages. An explanation for this might be overseas remittances where a family member who has gone overseas to live sends money to enable the family to upgrade their wooden house.

Local Housing

It's said that early colonists did not venture very deeply into Cameroon because the Monday to Monday, removing large trees from forest was so thick, they found it to be impenetrable. This reality was still obvious, and there are concerns in some quarters relating to the logging operations, which seem to run the forest.

Lumber being transported out of the forest

Cameroon is the leading exporter of timber products in Africa. This success brings with it an annual deforestation rate of 1%. Here, good management of the environment is vital. Cameroon has good laws which, unfortunately, at times are weakly enforced. Seems like I have said that before, referring to another part of the world.

In this town, and in the much larger Bertoua, taxis are hard to come by. Instead, it is the moto that provides the transportation. It is not uncommon to see a driver with three adult passengers, all of whom are carrying a bundle of some sort.

That Tuesday, I had an early start and went to the bank for some cash. Every place I've visited in West Africa has been a cash economy. I have probably used my credit cards in their "normal" fashion a handful of times; and, of course, it means there are days when I am carrying around bundles of local currency. I walked around the town for a while, getting a feel for it. It has a sense of busyness enforced by the motorcade of moto taxis moving quickly through the streets.

I'd heard of a large rock formation in the forest that men were cutting to supply materials for building. Fancying a ride into the forest, I got a moto driver to take me there. We went a good way into the forest, riding for more than half an hour, before reaching this rock.

The rock in the forest

A very interesting sight. I was able to get some nice pictures of the forest and the evening sunset. I am still trying to get some stunning sunset shots but don't think I have succeeded yet.

On the Wednesday, I caught an early morning bus to travel 40 km to a neighbouring town and see the Lac de Leta and Mount Yanga. Leaving the bus depot, the skies started to predict that rain was definitely on the way. The ride was about 90 minutes and the rain held off for an hour, but eventually, it did come. Because it wasn't the rainy season, it was neither heavy nor long, but it was still coming down when it was time for me to exit the bus. Prior, I was lucky enough to share my seat with a young boy and his chicken!

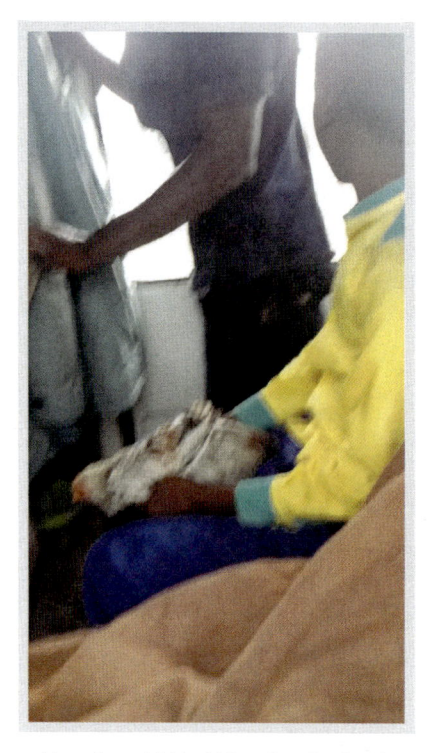

Young boy with his chicken along for the ride

If you were to look at a map you would see that the road I had been traveling on is a path cut out of the forest. It probably goes back centuries. All along the road were small villages without much indication that there was anything behind them other than more forest. When I got off, I had to quickly find a place to shelter until the rain had ended. While waiting, I was able to hire a moto to take me to the Leta Lake which was almost 4 km inland.

As soon as it was possible, we rode into the forest over a bumpy road, avoiding most of the large puddles the rain had created. Soon enough, we were there. What a beautiful sight! I was overwhelmed, as I hadn't expected it! Taking off my shoes, I stood in the water, which was warm. The moto rider explained that it was always warm. There were some small fish in the lake. In some places it was quite deep and in others quite shallow. It was a beautiful picnic setting, though it does require a 4 km hike if no motos are around.

Lac de Leta

Leaving the lake, we rode about 500 m and stopped to take pictures of Mount Yanga. It wasn't possible to ride up (unless you were an extreme sports participant) and I certainly didn't have the time to hike.

Mt. Yanga

However, I was able to get some nice pictures. After the adventure, it was back to the village of Leta where it was market day.

Some of the vendors come out from Bertoua and so, rather than waiting for an unscheduled bus, I was able to get in the car of a vendor who was heading back to the city. The plus was I was headed in the right direction. The minus was frequent stops to pick up foodstuffs going to Bertoua for sale.

By the time I got back to the city I was pretty hungry, so I went to the market and got some meat. There were many large grills used to cook the meat, and both beef and chicken were cooked on them. Additionally, there were ladies selling bakes. The ones I ate were beignets farine (which is made from flour), beignets de riz (which is made from rice), and beignets koki (which is made from koki beans. Koki beans are black eye beans). They each have a different taste, which I found difficult to describe.

Meat being cooked

TRIP INTO THE BUSH

I went into the bush the following day. This required a 40 km ride northeast of Bertoua. I had a conversation with a young man who sat beside me on the bus coming north from the capital city and he promised to take me into the bush while I was in Bertoua. So, today was to be the fulfillment of his promise. We drove, three on the bike, through this beautiful forest with its very stunning trees. I sat on the back of the moto for the entire ride while my new friend sat in the middle. The first stop was to see a place where, for many years, water had been seeping out of the rocks. However recently, unbeknownst to my young friend, the government has blocked the wall up in a way that the water falling could be controlled and provide a place for people to wash clothes. As a result, the miracle of water coming out of the rocks had come to an end.

We saw both cocoa and peppers growing in the wild. Cameroon has a good market for its peppers, while coffee production is very important to its economy. Believe it or not, Cameroon is the 30th largest coffee exporter in the world. In 2018 there were some 17 million coffee plants exported. Likewise, 220,000 tons of cocoa were exported. These products help diversify the economy.

Peppers

Many big trees had been felled in the area to make way for banana production. Sadly, the environment appeared to be falling behind the economic decisions, as Cameroon is the second highest exporter of bananas in Africa and the leading exporter of timber products in Africa.

Trees cut down by the loggers and left

We then walked along the road for a while before plunging into the bush. For the next hour, using a machete, my young guide carried us deeper in, searching for various trees. One such tree was a tall mango tree that grew smallish mangoes in clumps. All in all, it was a good experience, and no danger was encountered—no snakes or any other animals, for that matter.

When we decided it was time to head back, we called the rider and headed out of the bush. Seeing a man standing beside the road with a porcupine, we pulled over to take a picture of me holding it. Suddenly, a car pulled over, a man jumped out, ran up to me, grabbed the porcupine, took it to the guy who was selling it and bought it on the spot. He then jumped back into his car and drove off at top speed.

I'm still wondering what that was all about—and I didn't get my picture.

I should point out that in most areas where porcupines live, it's legal to hunt them as they are regarded as bushmeat.

As this was my last night in Bertoua, I joined my friend and a few of his friends for dinner in a location where bushmeat was sure to be available. We were in a very rustic setting and the waitress came and asked what we would like. Not having seen a menu, we asked what meats she had. To my delight, she named off a variety of bush meat, most of which I would not dare eat. However, she did name a type of antelope and that's what I ordered. It's worth mentioning that many people eat bush meat because they believe it to be healthier than processed meats. In Cameroon, the bushmeat includes antelope, chimpanzee, pangolin, elephant, gorilla, monitor lizard, porcupine, and snake.

Take your pick.

I expected the food preparation to take some time, so I got up and walked around. I was careful not to raise my phone, as I was sure I'd be spotted as a tourist and would have folk on me trying to sell all manner of things. Turning a corner, I saw an old lady with four dead monkeys at her feet. Our eyes met and she began her sales pitch, trying to sell me a monkey. Imagine that. I moved away as quickly as I could. As I continued looking around, I saw several dead animals that I couldn't imagine eating. After a while, I went back to the table. When the food came, I made every effort to eat my meat, but I didn't enjoy it very much (though I'm certain I ate more of the antelope than I would have eaten of the monkey)!

Chapter 3
Yaounde and Douala, Cameroon

"The only people who ever get anywhere interesting are those who get lost."
~Henry David Thoreau, 1817-1862—American poet and philosopher~

Up early, I headed back to the capital city. When I arrived up north just a few days ago, this scheduled five-hour trip took more than seven. I was very hopeful that it would be no more than six on this occasion. There was only one police stop in the first three hours and only four people were taken for inspection. I was lucky enough to be one of the few! When the officer spoke with me, he said, "Your documents are in order, but it will be a hot day. Can you provide beer money for the six of us?"

I replied by saying, "I hope you can find some cheap beers," and gave him 2,000 cfa.

Apart from this, it was a comfortable drive through the countryside. Pineapples and watermelon were in season, so at almost every roadside stand they were on display in great numbers. Currently, only about USD $6M is exported from the pineapple crop with the bulk of this going to France and Belgium. It is estimated that, due to a variety of reasons including poor farm-to-market methods, as much as 50% of fruit production is lost before it can be purchased.

Watermelon and pineapple stand

After two more hours, second police stop, this time the officer looked at my passport and asked where I was from. To keep things simple, I told him the UK. He then sent me about my business and didn't even look at my visa!

Back in the capital, the next day was a real touring day. I took a taxi for a four-mile drive to get to the first locale. Now, a four-mile taxi ride in Bermuda is serious money. Today it was my favourite request—two Mil which is USD 4. I went to the Benedictine Museum of Mont-Febe. This small museum is within a Catholic monastery, set upon a hill and providing a wonderful view of the city. If you let your mind wander back to colonial times, you can imagine the liaison between the colonial powers and the church. This site stirs up awkward memories.

The four-room museum had many very interesting pieces, but there was a no picture taking policy. This time, however, I broke the rule and took more than a few. The pieces are historical displays of the culture of the more significant tribes. The main items on display were bronze and wooden statues, ivory pipes, and tribal masks. Once I went outside, I took a seat and enjoyed the peace and calm that emanated from the place.

Artifacts from the museum

Artifacts from the museum

Walking for a while until I could get in a decent spot for getting a cab, I was able to take a few pictures looking back into the city. My next stop was the Jardin Zoo-Botanique de Mvog-Betsi, which is regarded as one of the best zoos in West Africa. This was a city zoo that had been opened in 1951. Sadly, it was in need of general maintenance, but the animals appeared to be in good condition (not that I know anything about animal health). One might consider that it's silly to go to Africa and visit a zoo, but there you have it! As it turned out, this small zoo had a variety of birds and animals, which included crocodiles, red river hog, lions, duiker (West African deer), baboons, turtles, snakes, various monkeys and the hard-to-spot-in-the-wild, mandrill. It was a place dedicated to children's enjoyment, so much so that there was a swimming pool as well!

Back on the moto, I next went to the Monument of Reunification. This was completed in 1973 to symbolise the vote taken by the people who lived in British Cameroon to join with French Cameroon. My understanding was that, in a free and fair vote, the people believed there should be one Cameroon exercised their democratic right to make it happen; however, 57 years later, some in the Anglophone sections of Cameroon were agitating to cede from Cameroon. The reason for this is said to be that most civil service jobs go to French Cameroon people and in many other aspects of life in Cameroon, the Anglophone are discriminated against. Despite this, the Government doesn't appear to have any interest in a free and fair vote like the vote of 1961.

Having said that, the monument was brilliant. First, there was a statue of an old man pulling in children. It's said that the old man represents those who had pushed for the reunification while the children represent those who will enjoy a better future in the reunified country. There was also the spiral tower, which rises from the ground in a circular manner and is designed in such a way you can walk inside to the top. Of course, I couldn't resist such an opportunity and up I went!

Monument of Reunification

Pleased with my day so far, I wanted to make one last stop: Place de l'independence. On January 1, 1960, the first Prime Minister of Cameroon, Ahmadou Ahidjo, formally proclaimed the freedom of the nation from France in this square. It had two statues of lions and two fountains, but the centerpiece is the 25 m high obelisk bearing the coat of arms of Cameroon. The square is often visited by school children and tourists and is still used on ceremonial occasions. This square is very special to the people of Cameroon. While there, a wedding party came to take pictures. I watched and clicked and even made a short video. It was very interesting to watch the wedding party as they celebrated the newlyweds. As part of the celebrations, it's customary for the bridal party to drive through the city with the girls sitting up on the side of the cars waving and singing.

It was time to leave the city and head for the coast. I wanted to see the city of Douala, which is the economic heart of the country. It is located right on the Atlantic and thus has been an important port city for at least the last five centuries. Because of this, it's the largest city in Cameroon.

My journey was on a lovely double-decker bus. The trip was expected to take four hours and cost a very reasonable USD $11. Each seat had a bottle of water waiting in a holster and during the journey a lady gave each passenger a choice of two sandwiches. I wished I'd been riding on that bus for the last year as I moved across West Africa! Music videos played throughout at a volume that was very comfortable. This might have been the most comfortable ride I'd had so far during my African journey.

Almost unbelievably, there was not one police check that day. Unfortunately, it felt like I'd entered another weather or climatic zone, and for the first time on the trip, I was thrust into the rainy season. As a result, after three hours of totally smooth sailing, we were suddenly in a torrential downpour. This continued unabated until we reached the bus depot in Douala.

So, with my suitcase and backpack, I needed to get to my hotel. Fortunately, the hotel wasn't too far away, but my only option for transport was a moto. With the rain pelting down and with heavy traffic all about, I gave my bag to a moto driver while I climbed on the back with my backpack. My prayers went up for our safety because it felt like as soon as we took off, the heavens really opened. I didn't have to worry about the driver taking me on a joyride to run up my bill, as he wanted to be rid of my bag as soon as possible! Later, I saw motos with umbrellas and wished I'd been on one of those.

After a short while, we were at the hotel, and I was freed from the rain. I was quickly processed and taken to the apartment I'd booked for this stay. What a nice surprise. The two-bedroom apartment was lovely with a kitchen, living room and dining room. There was even A.C. in the living room and the main bedroom—just what I needed to relax after the day's journey.

The next morning, I took a moto to Sandaga marche, as it was the greatest distance from the apartment and thus, I'd be working my way back after that. The market was huge with a variety of fruits and vegetables. There were people selling in large quantities like a large basket of tomatoes to those who had a dozen of them on a mat in front of them. One could spend a lot of time in the markets if trying to get a week's supply of fruit and vegetables. Because of the volume of produce, sellers from the smaller markets buy their supplies from here at what can be regarded as a wholesale price level then resell in their markets for profit. Apart from these food products there was little else. I did see some dried fish but not much more. I haven't yet eaten dried fish as I couldn't bring myself to do it. Of course, I wanted to snap away, but in that environment, I didn't feel comfortable pointing my camera so I didn't take a picture until I'd left the market and then took pictures from a distance.

I then walked to the Monument of New Liberty. Some say this is Cameroon's Statue of Liberty. It was created by a Cameroon artist over the lengthy period of ten years, between 1996 and 2007. The monument is made from recyclable materials such as tires, car parts and various metal pieces. Most of the pieces in the monument were gathered from various garbage dumps in the city. It is twelve meters high and weighs twenty tons. The sun wasn't cooperating with me, so I couldn't capture the work as I would have liked to. Soon after I'd taken a few pictures, the heavens opened, and I had to quickly find a place to shelter. The rain lasted about an hour, during which I could only sit and wait.

Monument of New Liberty

My next stop was the Akwa Palace Hotel. This is claimed to be the best hotel in the city and worth having a look. When I arrived, I went past security unchallenged and walked around the property before settling in an open seating area where I had a light lunch for probably three times what I would have paid in the street! The final stop for the day was the castle of King Akwa. I'm still unsure what the word *castle* means here, but to me it meant I would see the remains of a castle, or a castle being used for some other purpose. As a result, I never found the castle and was quite disappointed.

The next morning, I got a moto to take me to the Maritime Museum. Although the driver claimed to know where to go, it turned out he didn't know where the museum was, and instead of driving me to the museum, he drove into the docklands. His error was to my benefit, as I was able to see a huge dock. Clearly, Douala is the economic heart of Cameroon.

After some effort, we found the museum. This four-year-old museum is built in the shape of a boat and tells the story of the people and the sea for both Douala and Cameroon. The earliest people recorded here are the Sawa people who were from the Congo basin. They are said to have been established in the 15th century. The first exhibits showed their racing and war boats. The next showed the Rio Dos Camaroes, which was the name given to the river going into the ocean, which has a large number of shrimps in the river mouth. Today, many of the fishermen are from other nearby countries including Nigeria, which receives 30% of the fish caught there. Most of what remains is eaten nearby, while dried fish makes its way to inland markets.

I then looked at an exhibit about the slave ports of Limbe and Bimba. All the European nations in the slave trade took slaves from these two ports, so it's believed that people of Cameroonian descent can be found throughout the Diaspora. It's interesting to know that the slave port of Bimba had become forgotten in history even though it is now believed that very large numbers of Africans were sent to the New World from this port. From the 19th century, the main products going out from the Douala port were timber, rubber, palm oil and coffee, the last three of which had been introduced from South America.

Douala had been led by King Bell and Akwa tribes for more than 100 years. The Germans killed the kings in 1914, prior to their expulsion by the British and French. These deaths didn't sit well with the native population as the kings had been leading resistance against German rule. King Bell, who had been educated in Germany, pointed out that the Germans had violated the agreement of 1884 and attempted to legally force them to act within the agreement. Having little success going the legal route, he started to organize against the Germans, which eventually lead to his death.

In more recent times, there has been offshore oil exploration. Today this oil provides much income to the three neighbouring countries: Cameroon, Equatorial Guinea, and Gabon. There were exhibits detailing this very important economic aspect of Douala.

The last exhibit in the museum was the Storm Room. It tells the story of a native fighter, Malobe, who in the 1870s, tried to break the power of the colonialists. He was eventually caught, enslaved and sent to the New World. There's a simulation in which you sit in a small boat and experience the Middle Passage journey. For me, this was one of the most vivid experiences I've ever had learning about the slave trade. If you're ever in Cameroon, go to the Maritime Museum in Douala and experience this for yourself.

Having enjoyed the museum, I went looking for King Bell's palace and was quite disheartened when I found a restaurant operating out of it. Perhaps this was because I'd been expecting a statelier role for the king's former residence. Nevertheless, I could see its interesting design, which had been built by the Germans in 1905 for King Bell. Upon independence, this building was used as the House of Assembly.

Doual' Art is a small contemporary art studio. I saw it in passing and ducked in as the raindrops were getting more frequent. It rained for the next hour while I sat there and enjoyed their lovely garden. The artwork was beautiful and most had been done by local artists. This was the organization which had funded the Monument of New Liberty and is currently run by a member of King Bell's family.

As Douala was one of the earliest cities in Cameroon and was the place from which the Germans governed, I then went in search of historic houses. I eventually found three. The first is currently used by the Chamber of Commerce. The second is a government building across the street, but I was unable to determine which government department occupied the building. The third, which was a few blocks away, was the stateliest of the three, giving me the impression it had to have been a very important building in its heyday. Unfortunately, it's very much in a state of disrepair. Various vendors were selling their goods outside of the unused building. I did some research and found that, sure enough, it had been one of the grander buildings during the German era, but it hadn't been owned or built by the Germans. The house, known as Villa Mandessi-Bell, was built in 1904 by David Mandessi-Bell, a rich native farmer who lived in it until his death in 1936. This house is typical of the German and colonial style architecture of the period.

Villa Mandessi-Bell

My last stop for the day was the Cathedral of Saints Peter and Paul. The Cathedral was striking and had an unusual wooden ceiling. This is the main Catholic church in Douala and was completed in 1936 during the French colonial period.

Cathedral of Saints Peter and Paul

Cameroon tradesmen. The materials are all produced in Cameroon and, where the product is being made on spec, the furniture sits here by the road day in and day out. Also, each night everything must be covered and when it rains, the men move quickly to protect it. When a customer finally purchases the furniture, it's given a thorough cleaning before delivery.

Beautiful furniture produced by local craftsmen

Beautiful furniture produced by the local craftsmen

Douala is the only place I've travelled to in Africa where I've been caught in the rainy season. So, what does a moto driver do in the rainy season? He puts an umbrella on his bike! It's common to see the rider carrying his passenger under the cover. As I walked along, I saw many of these umbrellas for sale, and they were certainly very colourful.

Chapter 4
Kirbi, Cameroon

"I haven't been everywhere but it's on my list."
~Susan Sontag 1933-2004—American writer, philosopher, and political activist~

I got up early in the morning in Douala, organized myself, and was out the door. The bus going to Kribi was right around the corner, so it only required a few strides for me to be inside the building buying my ticket at 9:45 AM. To my surprise, the bus I'd passed going into the building was the one going to Kribi. So, I had to get right on and was rewarded with a seat at the very back, but I didn't need to endure the one-, two-, three-hour wait for enough people to fill the bus. I had to take my suitcase onto the bus and the ticket handler took the bag and made space for it in the overhead bin. We were on the go by 10:05 AM.

The bus was full. There must have been at least 50 people on it, but we made little headway. An hour after leaving the depot we had gone 18 km! Why? I had no idea. After two hours, we'd traveled 44 km—and we were on excellent roads. The road was very busy during this time and half an hour later, we were at 66 km. I'd been told that this was a two-hour trip, yet after two and a half hours, we'd just reached halfway. At this point, I was starting to get a little irritated. Fortunately, there was a wonderful landscape to enjoy. Soon after, we came upon an old bridge at a place called Eden, I *had* to take pictures of this bridge. This steel arch bridge was designed and built by the Germans and shipped to Cameroon in 1911. At 160 m in length, it was the largest bridge in Africa at the time of its construction.

Eden Bridge

Finally, we arrived at our first stop. Many of the men jumped off for the open-air lavatories. Ladies came on the bus selling their wares. I bought some banana chips and then decided I should get something a little more substantial. A lady was selling beef in a stew inside baguettes, so I decided to get one. By this time, most people were back on the bus and the driver was revving up the engine. This lady worked as quickly as she could to complete my baguette, but lo and behold, the driver took off before she could. The startled lady worked her way to the front as quickly as she could. People were shouting to the driver, but he ploughed on until he'd gone about half a mile then stopped and let her off.

How mean! And the baguette was delicious.

Soon after it started to rain. I was worried that the heavy rains experienced in Douala would be repeated, but luckily it only lasted a short while. Up until that point, there'd been no police security checks. This was surprising given where we were. Finally, we were almost at our destination and a police check came. Unlike the others, it was very relaxed; so much so, the officer who dealt with me invited me to enjoy my stay in Cameroon.

Having arrived close to 3 PM, I needed a taxi to take me the 11 km to the hotel. It was too far to expect a moto driver to balance my bag on his gas tank! After settling in, I went down to the beach and relaxed. It was a pleasant setting with many who appeared to be locals and a few tourists. While there, I watched the France versus Peru World Cup match—not a bad performance by Peru, as they only lost 1-0. By the time the match ended, the sun was setting and I took several sunset shots before walking back to the hotel.

I think I'm getting closer to capturing that evasive great shot!

Kribi sunset

The hotel in which I was staying was only a few meters from Lobe Beach. That morning after breakfast, I went to swim and have a look at the famous waterfall. The beach water appeared dirty but was nice to swim in—and it wasn't too rough. I was made to understand that the colouring is due to there being a volcanic seabed. I didn't go up to the falls in a boat, (something I'd do later during my stay) but I did get some good pictures.

Later on, I went to the fish market to have lunch. The set up was that you purchased your fish before taking it to one of the grill stations where it was cooked. This meant your fish could be as fresh as the last boat that had come in. When the plate returned, the fish was tasty and served with sliced plantain. While waiting (and it was a wait), more boats came in with their catch. I saw a few lobsters and decided I'd definitely have one before I left Kribi.

I left full and headed for the market in town. I went through the town but didn't see anything of interest before going back to my hotel. Later, I got a plate of shrimp and plantain for dinner. The shrimp was delicious.

Kribi market

Did you know the name *Cameroon* is a derivative of the Portuguese word for 'shrimp'? Fernando Po, a Portuguese explorer, gave the name in 1472, as he found the estuary to Douala to be full of it, so he named it the Rio des Camaros, translated river of the shrimps.

There are 40,000 pygmies in various parts of Cameroon. This represents approximately 20% of all the pygmies in Africa. They usually live deep in the rain forests in isolation. These hunter-gatherers are semi-nomadic and usually avoid outside contact. In Kribi, there are three villages "upriver". The tribes in this area have a high degree of contact with the outside world, so the primitive aspects of tribal life are changing. Having decided to go to visit the pygmy settlement, I was told I should present the pygmies with a gift, which I was happy to do. I was then told I could take either a large bag of rice or a carton of cigarettes. I was disgusted by the second choice, not so much for health reasons but for cultural purity reasons.

I made arrangements to go up the river Lobe to a pygmy village named Namicombi. To do this, I had to get to the point of departure. One of the tribesmen guided a small canoe for two km to the village. I could see another canoe ahead of us with five or six people in it. To my delight, along the way we saw some small monkeys darting through the trees.

When we arrived, there were many small children in a village of forty people. The chief, whom I met, was a traditional medicine man. Because of his knowledge, people from Kribi and other nearby villages come to him for treatment. The people, who average four feet in height, live a very simple life. They don't have electricity, so the luxuries electricity brings are foreign to them. Their diet consists of breadfruit, cassava, corn as well as fish, chicken, turtles, and bush meats.

Pygmy children helping secure our boat

Due to the size of pygmy communities, no one is allowed to marry inside the village. As a result, the hopeful husband must find a potential wife from among other villages. Once achieved, he must produce the bride price, which is usually bush meat, honey, and palm wine.

I don't make a habit of visiting tribes and primitive people. This is because I'm not comfortable sticking my camera in these people's faces. While I was there, the other group I'd seen on the river were there as well. I was annoyed when I noticed one man with a large professional camera go right up to an older woman and snap her picture, face-on. Because I feel the way I do, my pictures of the adult pygmies are few, although I do have more of the children.

I didn't know what to make of the experience. I saw a small village of people who appeared to be living in abject poverty. The children's clothes were (to be polite) not nice. The village itself was dirty and the huts I looked into were extremely messy. Worse still, there were many empty cigarette boxes littering the area in which we landed. And I say this not to judge but to wonder whether these native people's day-to-day lives need to be exposed to tourists at all. Again, we must question what qualifies as cultural tourism and what doesn't and discard those activities which are culturally demeaning.

Pygmy village

The following day I toured the Kribi area by taxi and saw a nice mix of houses, wooden and block. I got the impression that the earnings from tourism and other means were working their way through the entire community. There was much new construction to see, both commercial and residential.

Kribi was at the time of my visit the site of the construction of a deep-water seaport. There was much work going on to build an attractive warehousing area, supported by Chinese funding. Unlike many other Chinese funded projects, it appeared that this one was using a mostly Cameroonian workforce, supported by three hundred Chinese workers. Landscaping was in full steam. Plants were to be built. Upon completion, the port became the largest dry-water port in Central Africa. The estimated cost of the project was $1.1B euros, with the Chinese government providing 85% of the funding. As a result, it's being overseen by the China Harbor Engineering Corporation. This project has been very successful and the new port has proven to be a huge economic boost for both Kribi and the country.

As usual, I was taking pictures when two workers shouted, "No pictures." I smiled because this was a country with very strong state controls, and this was how those controls actually played out. As a result, despite the fact that my photos would do no harm, there was a request that I stop, and so I did.

Construction of the new port

The road to Campo, where one would cross into Equatorial Guinea by boat, was approximately 45 km away. I'd planned to visit Equatorial Guinea on this trip, but apart from the fact that costs are really high for tourists and that there frankly isn't that much for an island-boy to see, the government simply doesn't want tourists and makes obtaining a visa extremely difficult. Because of this, I was forced to simply stop trying. This country is ranked as the least visited country in the world by tourists. It had only one hundred and fifty tourists in 2016—a very closed society.

Having had enough excitement, I went swimming at Plage de Grande Batanga, one of the 'nice beaches' in the area. This sandy beach is 6 km long. There the Atlantic Ocean waves were very strong and I got knocked over more than once. After I got tired of the ocean beating me up, I had lunch which consisted of crabs and fish. The crabs were so fresh I could still taste the salt on them! Then, it was back up the coastline to Lobe Beach to watch a World Cup match.

Tasty shrimp meal at the seaside

The next day I went to Lobe beach again. My lunch consisted of fish and shrimp and was very tasty. Once again, it was a slow delivery (taking more than two hours), but hey—I'm not on the clock, so I decided to lay back and enjoy it! In addition to the very nice (but slow and expensive) restaurant, there was an area set aside for artisans to share and sell their work on the dock. I spent some time looking at the artwork along with some woodwork, which was very well done.

The time had finally come for me to do the full Lobe Falls experience. I took a boat up to Chutes de lobe or Lobe Waterfall. This is what I had come to Kribi to see. This waterfall was located at the point where the inland river Lobe meets the Atlantic. It's one of the few places in the world where a freshwater waterfall empties into a saltwater ocean. The closest to this is the Dunn River Falls in Jamaica, which many Bermudians (including myself) have enjoyed. While swimming a few days ago, I *tasted* the water as it slammed up against me. When I was a distance away from the Falls, the water was salty (as was to be expected) but as I got closer to it, I could taste fresh water!

While having my relaxing lunch, I'd watched two groups of people go up to the Falls in the small boat used by the guide. It looked exciting, sort of like the Maid in the Mist at Niagara Falls. I readily confess that I never rode in the Maid in the Mist, and I never will. It just looks too dangerous. That day, however, I didn't feel apprehensive, so after lunch I had a go! The pictures show my boat going very close to these beautiful Falls.

Lobe Waterfalls

Lobe Waterfalls

BACK TO THE CAPITAL, YAOUNDE

I said goodbye to the staff at my small hotel and headed for the bus depot close to 10 AM. Kribi is one of the two most popular beach towns in Cameroon. It's attractive with enough to do if you know where to look, but boy was it expensive! Constant negotiations were necessary to avoid giving away every penny I had.

There were two bus companies with buses going to the city. One bus looked fuller than the other but when I queried, I was told all the seats had been sold.

No quick ride out of town.

I went to the other bus and, after getting a ticket, climbed on not long after 10 AM, but we had to wait for the bus to fill, so departure was delayed until 11:25 AM.

Within one hour, there was a police check that was very routine and excitement-free. The ladies by the side of the road were selling boiled eggs and dried fish. I decided to sample the eggs but still wasn't ready to try the dried fish. This bus wasn't as nice as other buses I have ridden on in Cameroon, and so my last bus ride was in a bus with no A.C. and few windows. Help! It's stifling!

We stopped for some unknown reason and the driver would not let any vendors on. Crazy.

Vendors left at the roadside

About fifteen minutes later, we stopped again. This time five vendors came on, but he drove off without letting them off until we were about half a mile up the road! This is not the chicken bus experience of Central America. There, at almost every stop for the long-distance buses, vendors would stream on selling all manner of items. The drivers would welcome them and ensure they were able to do some business before having to get off.

Happy vendors on the bus

Eventually, we arrived in the city. I had to take a taxi and a moto back to my old hotel. Easier going back there than to find my way to a new place. After relaxing, I went to get a good meal at a reasonable cost (i.e., not Kribi prices!) and watch a World Cup match on a big screen.

The National Museum of Cameroon is said to be one of the best in Africa and I really wanted to tour it. This day would be my third attempt. I was glad to have been so determined. This museum was first class. Compared to other points of interest in Cameroon, where most often there was no entry fee, this place was expensive at almost USD $10; but it was worth it.

It's a large, elegant building which was the home of the first president of independent Cameroon. Like the UK House of Parliament, where Mr. Speaker has living quarters, one wing of the building was the president's home while the Cabinet room and other important offices occupied the rest of the building. This was so from 1961 until the president resigned in 1982. The following and present president moved the government elsewhere. As a result, this building became unused for some years before opening as the National Museum in 1988.

Museum

I was fortunate to have a guide who enjoyed his work. He took me around the building for two hours, showing and educating me on Cameroon culture and history. The museum had over one thousand artifacts from the ten different regions. While there, I didn't see other people who appeared to be visitors. The grounds were attractive and the bronze statues set off the place. There were also twelve fountains and an exhibit by artists from the Congo, which reflected the similarities of the culture of the countries in the region.

Next was a display of habitats across the country along with clothing typical of each of the regions. It was very interesting to see how the living conditions adapted across the country. Then followed the masks and instruments of war in the regions. The masks are fantastic to see. Again, I was so disappointed that I wasn't allowed to take pictures, as I am unable to adequately describe everything I saw. A picture is worth a thousand words! The last of the cultural displays were musical instruments of many types and sizes. Not to be forgotten was the display of artifacts going back to the Iron and Stone ages.

Display inside the museum

We examined the history of the independent Cameroon on a decade-by-decade basis. This highlighted many of the successes of the nation. Lastly, before leaving, I was shown a presentation of the slave trade tying together Cameroon, France and Britain, and Antigua and Barbuda. As part of the presentation, Bermudian slave, Mary Prince was featured showing the part her story played in ending the slave trade.

Outside of the museum

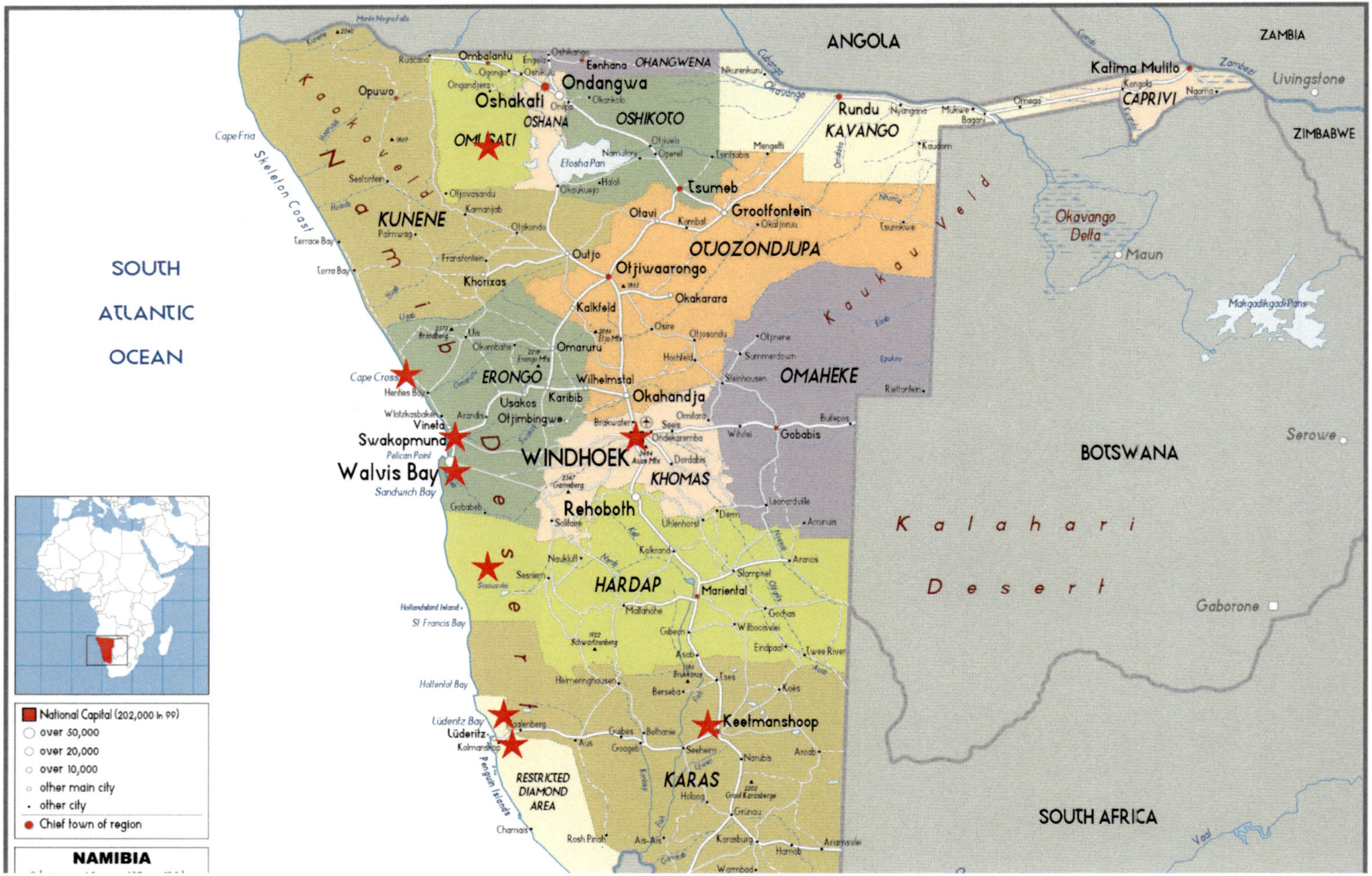
ANGOLA
ZAMBIA
ZIMBABWE
BOTSWANA
SOUTH AFRICA
SOUTH ATLANTIC OCEAN
Kalahari Desert
Namib Desert
Kaokoveld
Kaukauveld
Okavango Delta
Makgadikgadi Pans
Etosha Pan
Skeleton Coast
Cape Fria
Cape Cross
Pelican Point
Sandwich Bay
Hollandsbird Island
St. Francis Bay
Hottentot Bay
Lüderitz Bay
Penguin Islands
Livingstone
Maun
Serowe
Gaborone
KUNENE
OMUSATI
OSHANA
OHANGWENA
OSHIKOTO
KAVANGO
CAPRIVI
OTJOZONDJUPA
OMAHEKE
ERONGO
KHOMAS
HARDAP
KARAS
RESTRICTED DIAMOND AREA
WINDHOEK
Walvis Bay
Swakopmund
Oshakati
Ondangwa
Rundu
Katima Mulilo
Tsumeb
Grootfontein
Otjiwarongo
Okahandja
Rehoboth
Keetmanshoop
Mariental
Gobabis
Lüderitz
Opuwo
Outjo
Khorixas
Omaruru
Usakos
Otjimbingwe
Karibib
Wilhelmstal
Kalkfeld
Okakarara
Otavi
Ombalantu
Eenhana
Vineta
National Capital (202,000 in 99)
over 50,000
over 20,000
over 10,000
other main city
other city
Chief town of region
NAMIBIA

Chapter 5
Windhoek

"The journey is my home."
~Unknown~

Goodbye to Cameroon.
 Hello to Namibia
I'd been forced to improvise over the past three weeks. My original travel plans included one week in Gabon, followed by one in Cameroon, and then one in Equatorial Guinea before going back to Gabon for another week and finally heading to Namibia. *That* was the plan; but I couldn't get a visa for Equatorial Guinea. I was not destined to be one of the one hundred and fifty people per year who get to be a tourist in that country! If you don't believe this, you can research it—and while I can tell you that figure, I cannot tell you why a country with very modern hotels would not want tourists in them!

My week in Gabon was more costly than previous visits to African nations and returning to Gabon by road would take two full days. So, if I went back for a week, I'd actually get five very expensive days as opposed to seven in less costly Cameroon. Because of this analysis, one week in Cameroon became three. The most interesting thing about this was that due to the serious unrest in the Anglophone area of the country, I couldn't go there. It would have been easy to spend a week there doing things I would have enjoyed. Unfortunately, it wasn't an option.

So, my first month was over.

Namibia has been described as an upper middle-income country. There's a standard of wealth across the nation that isn't enjoyed across all classes of the people. In fact, Namibia is said to have the second worst income disparity in the world behind South Africa.

The income is generated from minerals such as diamonds, uranium, gold, and copper. GDP per capita is relatively high at USD$5,842. Almost 50% of exports go to neighbouring countries, such as South Africa, Botswana, and Zambia. Offsetting this success is an unemployment rate of 34%. The South West Africa People's Organisation (SWAPO), the government since independence, had promised jobs and opportunities for the native population as well as land and housing, but these promises remain undelivered.

The official language is English, although thirteen languages are recognised as national languages. The religion of the country is Christianity, which is followed by over 80% of the people. There is free schooling in the seven years of primary school, but unfortunately only 20% of students go on to higher education. Despite this, the literacy rate is 92%.

I was attracted to the diverse nature of the country from Etosha National Park in the north, to Cape Cross on the Atlantic Ocean, to the Namib desert and the great sand dunes. I could hardly wait to see these places!

I got up early and went to the airport using a moto then a taxi. The drive seemed to take forever but it was only twelve miles to reach the airport, so I arrived really early. After a few small bumps, I was seated comfortably in the departure area with about ten other passengers. While researching this trip, I came across a story on the Internet that said the airline provides a voucher for hotel and dinner for any passenger who has a scheduled layover longer than eight hours. Mine was scheduled to be twelve. So, I qualified for the voucher. At that point, no one had said a word about it and I was looking at the prospect of having to sleep in a chair at the airport overnight. Mind you, it wouldn't be the first time—I'd done it in October 2016 in the Suriname airport on my way back to Rio. I decided to ask when I checked, only for the lady to rudely tell me to go outside to someplace which, after asking twice, I still didn't know the name of! I left anyway, as I'd obviously used up my time with her.

Once I got outside, I immediately saw the Ethiopia airline office. I went in and was told that the vouchers would be issued at the gate at the time of boarding. So, I sat at the gate and waited with ten other people.

Time passed. I asked about the vouchers and was told they'd come. Eventually the plane started to load... no voucher for me. The more I asked, the sillier the responses became, so I didn't budge. Eventually, I was the only passenger left in the departure area, and I refused to move. The lady in charge pleaded with me to board, promising that the voucher would be brought to my seat. Of course, I was not happy. I didn't want to miss my flight. I didn't want to be escorted to the detention center at the airport (assuming there was one), but still I didn't want to move. Surrendering to the fact that this good thing was not going to happen for me, I started to board and just then my voucher arrived.

Lister makes sure he gets on the flight!

My routing may appear strange. I was going from *Central* West Africa to Southwest Africa. Both countries share the Atlantic coastline, yet I was flying 3,000 km east to Ethiopia and the following day, 3,700 km back to Southwest Africa. This happened because, having decided which countries I was going to, this flight on Ethiopian Airlines was the only way for me to get to where I wanted to be. This was my first flight on Ethiopian Airlines and the ground staff had certainly gotten it off on a bad start; however, that was turned around onboard.

We had a smooth flight with a tasty meal, comfortable seats, and attentive staff. What more can you ask for? Over the past few years, from time to time, I've read negative articles about this airline. I reject them all. Since this flight, I have flown three more times with them, and I was satisfied every time. I strongly recommend flying Ethiopian Airlines, as they had an "aim to please attitude", which I found very pleasing along with the good meals and high quality tv system.

On the ground at 9 PM-ish, I quickly made my way to the immigration area. In preparing for this flight, I read that I'd need an e-visa to leave the airport. I passed a small number of people who were at an e-visa counter and wondered if I should join them. Not wanting to wait, I decided to go on. Good decision as when I got to the counter the officer looked at my passport and asked for the following day's boarding pass and hotel voucher. Seeing these, I was processed. I wanted to get a sim card but after being unable to find anyone to register my phone, I decided not to bother. It wasn't needed as the only time I was going to be offline was the journey to and from the airport.

As it turned out, the airport is in the city! Traveling from the airport to the hotel took no more than ten minutes. Because it was so close, I didn't take pictures going or coming. I hadn't given much thought to how close or far from the city the airport would be, as almost every airport is a good distance from the city. I was happily surprised that the hotel we were put in was a very nice one and my room was good. On top of that, the choice of dinners was more than acceptable. This made the voucher deal a great side-benefit.

I'd set my alarm for 6 AM, as the shuttle bus was scheduled to leave at 6:30 AM; however, I got a wakeup call at 5:35 AM, telling me breakfast was ready. I hadn't expected breakfast as the time was so early and the voucher had said dinner with no mention of any other meal; but having been invited, I got myself together and went.

Earlier, I'd heard other people on my floor moving around, so I assumed I would see them at breakfast, but the room was empty when I got there. There was a full breakfast buffet, which was very inviting. I noticed a section with Ethiopian foods, so I selected these items. Why not try Ethiopian cuisine? Who knows when my travels will bring me to Ethiopia again.

Once done at 6:15 AM, I checked out of the hotel and sat to wait for the bus. I had left four people in the breakfast room. Within a short time, the shuttle driver returned and picked me up only, so l realised that this had to have been done with the people who l had heard earlier. It took only minutes before l was inside the terminal and at 8:35 AM, I was on my way to Namibia.

I had a pleasant four-hour flight to Hosea Kutako International Airport in Windhoek. The airport is named after one of the country's national heroes. When I got into the arrivals hall, I found that very few of the passengers were locals. Instead, most of us were in the visitors' line. Unfortunately, this meant that it took me well over an hour to get out of the hall. Even though Namibia is a no visa requirement destination for EU passport holders, I still couldn't get out of there in a reasonable amount of time.

Once out, I had to get some local currency. I went to an ATM that wasn't working.

Hmmm.

I was directed to a Standard bank atm. I tried more than one credit card, but all were rejected. At that point, I was becoming a little frustrated. A man approached offering taxi services. I asked the cost of his service, and he quoted the very figure I'd been advised to pay—but I still needed cash and a SIM card. He directed me to a working machine, but the most one could withdraw at one time was N$3000, which is just USD $225! As there were people now lining up behind me, I took my small fortune and headed for the SIM card. I explained that I would be in the country for a month, and the guy sold me a SIM for the large sum of N$7 and then a package for N$160. Remember, this is for a month's cellphone usage. In US dollars, this package totalled USD $12.

On my way!

The airport is 45 km from Namibia's capital city, Windhoek. We drove through scrublands where local farmers were keeping their cattle, though I must confess, I didn't see any cattle. We drove parallel to a small mountain range, the Auas mountains, which having a range of 56 km, runs like a spine right to the city.

Driving from the airport heading for Windhoek

Upon arrival at my small guesthouse, I found that they had two locations and I was going to be at the other one nearby. I walked to the second locale alongside two ladies from their staff and dropped my things before journeying into the city with the ladies who were kind enough to take me so I could get my bearings.

First impressions: Windhoek is beautiful, modern with an old-town charm. It's also clean. I was amazed at how tidy it was. Nothing I'd previously seen in Africa compared. I was looking forward to my stay.

Clocktower

On my first day in beautiful Namibia, I walked into the city and started with a visit to the Bushman Art gallery and museum. This is both a shop selling the work of the Bushmen and a private museum with historical pieces. The museum had African masks, carvings, weapons, musical instruments, walking sticks and jewelry. Today, the Bushmen are very few in number There are only 27,000 in Namibia and they live in very remote parts of the country. I was impressed with what I saw in both the items for sale and the delightful artifacts in the museum but I didn't take pictures as it didn't seem to be the right thing to do when some of the items were "for sale" items.

I left there and walked through a small city park on the way to the German Lutheran Church. This is a historic landmark in Windhoek that unfortunately, isn't open often to the public, so I joined the small group of picture takers. It was officially opened in 1910, four years before the Germans were expelled. It's interesting to think that this church, built by the Germans, has been in existence for over one hundred years, yet the builders only had use of it for four.

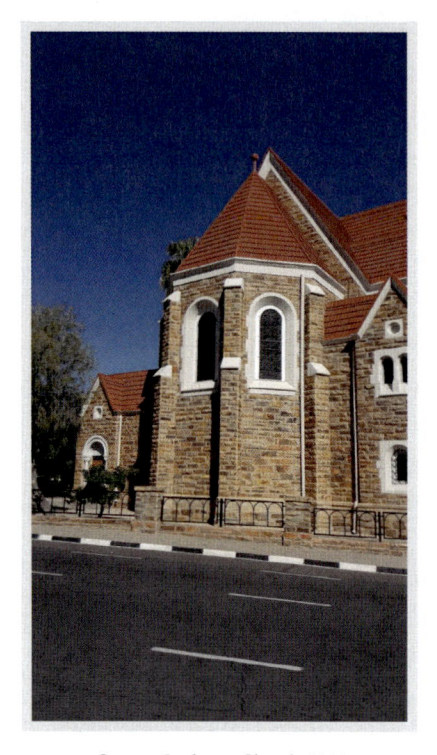

German Lutheran Church, 1910

Actually, this statement is incorrect. Even though the German government was expelled, many Germans remained and today, German Namibians represent 5% of the country's population of 2.5 million people. Additionally, they own and operate a significant proportion of the large farms in the country.

The church borders the Parliamentary Gardens. These lovely grounds, created in 1932, are always open to the public. In the gardens, there are three statues of past Namibian heroes, including Hosea Kutako. I then went up to the House of Parliament, though because it was the weekend, the House was closed. There was a security officer who responded to my friendly wave with one of his own, so I proceeded to take a few pictures.

Parliament grounds

Next was the moving Museum of Independence, which documents the fight for the independence of this nation; however, before entering the museum, I stood in front of the giant statue of Dr. Sam Nujamo who, as leader of SWAPO, led the fight for independence from 1960 to 1990. He became the country's first president and is still alive today at the ripe old age of eighty-eight years old.

Dr. Sam Nujamo

As mentioned, the museum tells the story of the native people and Namibia's fight for independence. The story starts from the 1880s, showing the actions of the Germans in putting down attempts to remove them. There were many pictures highlighting the torture and execution of some fighters. Later sections of the museum SWAPO's' fight to bring independence from South Africa.

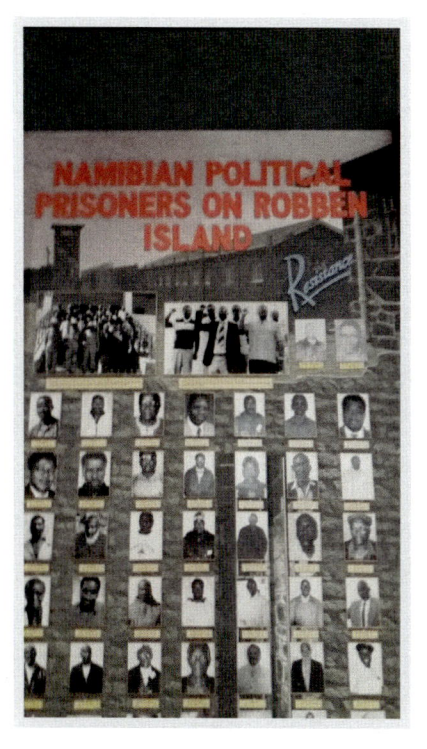

Namibian prisoners of war

I was surprised to learn that some of their fighters were imprisoned on Robben Island, some for as long as nineteen years. UN resolution #435 recommended the freedom of the country from South Africa in 1983 but, despite this, independence was delayed until 1990. This museum is a must-see for anyone traveling to Namibia.

There were three castles built in the downtown section of Windhoek. I went out the following day to see them and to learn about their history. While I thought the castles had been built in some earlier time (1700s maybe) I was surprised to learn they were all built in the early 1900s by one man, Wilhelm Sander, a German architect. At no point did these castles serve any military purpose. Instead, initially they were all private residences.

I walked to a hill called Lover's Point where I could look over the city. The first castle, named Schwerinsburg Castle, was at this point; however, it's now the home of the Italian ambassador and there was a security officer, who, doing his job, made sure I understood I couldn't enter the grounds. I could see parts of the original castle but was not allowed entry! Despite this, I was able to take pictures from that point and later from another vantage point I took a few more.

Schwerinsburg Castle

I then walked to Heinitzburg Castle. This was built in 1914. Originally Sander built this castle for himself but sold it two years later and the new owner named it after his wife. Today, the castle is an elegant hotel and restaurant.

Heinitzburg Castle

Next, I walked into what was very much a private residential neighbourhood. Again, still high on a hill, the views were amazing. I reached the third castle known as Sanderburg, which was completed by 1919 by Sander, again as his own residence. This is the smallest of the three castles. Sadly, Sander only lived there for two years before moving to the south of the country to a town called Lüderitz. I'll share more about Lüderitz later.

Sanderburg Castle

Chapter 6
Swakopmund

"Jobs fill your pocket but adventures fill your soul."
~Jamie Lyn Beatty, 1987—American actress~

I left Windhoek and travelled cross country to the oceanside city of Swakopmund. Before going, I got a new SIM card, as the one I purchased at the airport no longer had credit. When I went to recharge it, I learnt that I'd simply been with the wrong cell company, and I would have trouble getting a Wi-Fi signal in the desert. As a result, I switched to the biggest and best cell company —MTC.

My impression of Windhoek was positive. The parts of the city I saw were clean and the shops were modern, yet history had been captured and promoted as well. Most importantly, the people had a positive air about them.

The shuttle was unlike any other I've ridden in West Africa. The very clean vehicle had five passengers and six seats; however, like in West Africa, it had a "leave when full" policy. So, we waited for our final passenger. The fare was reasonable considering I was taking a 361 km, four-hour journey along the Naukluft mountain range at a cost of USD $11. As we were approaching Swakopmund, we passed the Rossing uranium mine, which is said to be the second largest uranium mine in the world. The driver pointed out that there are tours of the mine and I made a note to take a tour while there.

The drive was through the desert with open land and made for magnificent scenery. The vehicle stopped at the drop point outside the town where I saw solar panels on top of single-story buildings, right on the edge of the city. After a good day where all had gone well, my taxi driver didn't know how to get to my hotel. My blood rose very quickly as the hotel was right on the ocean, opposite the National Aquarium. I showed him how to get there on *maps.me* but this was no help. Finally, I called the hotel, and the staff told him how to get there.

Taxi drivers are the bane of my existence!

When I got going the next day, I walked to the waterfront to see how rough the water was. That day, it was serious. I went over to the historic jetty which extends out into the Atlantic. From the jetty there are great views (on a good day) back into the city and along the beachfront. The jetty was built in 1905 as both a cargo and passenger landing site. On a good day, the jetty is buzzing with tourists who enjoy the views then eat at one of the two restaurants at either end. The wind was so strong that as I went back, the water blew right up to the wooden planks.

Swakopmund is full of German architecture and there is a significant German presence in the city.

Rough seas at Swakopmund

I then walked two blocks to the snake park. This small place, which is a converted city home, has several snakes from Namibia as well as neighbouring countries, such as Botswana and Angola. The snakes are kept in glass cases, which makes easy viewing and provides a feeling of safety for those nervous around snakes. There are both harmless snakes and those which are most venomous. Plenty of information was provided about each, including toxicity, life span and habitat. There are ninety species of snakes of which eleven can deliver a lethal bite. Three of these were in the snake park: the cape cobra, the black mamba, and the puffer adder. There was also a fair size monitor lizard in the backyard moving freely about. Fortunately, it paid me no mind.

The uninterested monitor lizard

That Wednesday, I made a trip to Cape Cross which is 120 km north. This is the only place in the world where you find the
Cape fur seal. My driver collected me at 9:30 AM, and we travelled along the coastline. In doing so, we passed a few small towns. As usual, the Atlantic Ocean was very rough, so I saw no swimmers at any point.

After about an hour, we slowed down as a stretch of the road was being rebuilt. Later, we saw one of the few tourists highlights along the way, the shipwrecked Zeila that went down close to shore in 2008. The ship was sold to Indian investors who were going to take it to India, but it broke loose and came ashore near Henties Bay where it remains. Today, washed up on the beach, it gives folks a good photo stop. I should mention that this area and going north on the coast is called the Skeleton Coast. This name was given due to the number of shipwrecks along this coastline over many years. It is estimated that there are over 1,000 ships underwater along the Skeleton Coast; however, we didn't stop, as I was keen to get to the Cape Cross reserve.

Next, we passed Henties Bay, which is a small town filled with retirees and vacationers who want to be on the water. We were driving in the Dorab national park, which runs just north of Cape Cross to just south of Swakopmund. This is another vast desert area. To my surprise, I saw salt flats. I had no idea that the Namibians worked salt flats! I later learned that there are similar salt works at Walvis Bay and exports from the port there total one million tons annually, making Namibia the world's 30th largest salt producer. We were now driving on salted roads. The use of salt hardens the road more quickly, but it's very slippery when wet. Additionally, the coastal roads are subject to mist and fog at certain times of the year also. This occurs most often at night and as a result, there are many accidents during that time. We finally entered through the Cape Cross reserve through the Ugab River gate at 11:30 AM, after covering the 120 km in two hours—not bad under the circumstances. There was very little traffic and there was no public transport along this road. All tourists and other visitors must book a tour and hire a driver if they're going to participate in it. There was an admission fee of 80 Namibian dollars per person (USD $6).

What a sight was waiting for me! The Cape Cross reserve is the home of up to 200,000 seals. It's home to the largest breeding colony of fur seals in the world. Truly an amazing sight to behold. I initially viewed the seals from a long walkway. Later, I got my nerve up and walked among them. There were so many lying in the sun but even more were in the water enjoying the large waves. One of their distinctive features is that, unlike other seals, these have external ears. These seals don't migrate, but they have been found over 1,000 km away and as far out at sea as 200 km! A big reason for traveling so far is their diet. These seals feed off squid, octopus, sharks, and stingrays.

Seals, seals and more seals!

One thing that cannot be avoided at the reserve is the smell. The combination of excrement and dead seals creates a horrible odor. Sick and young seals are preyed upon by hyenas and jackals. I had to fight to keep the smell from upsetting my tummy. In addition, there was the noise. It was amazing how much noise the seals made. Just watch a video on YouTube and you'll hear what I mean!

Cape Cross has historic significance as well. In 1386, a Portuguese navigator, Diego Cao, landed at this spot. He put a stone cross into the rock to mark his landing. Today, a replica is in its place. As a history buff myself, I took a couple of pictures of this. Because Cao was wise enough to mark his landing, this area is a National Heritage site.

After having a good visit, we headed back towards Swakopmund and I was surprised to see a line of stands at the roadside with some form of crystal. Although no one was around working these stands, we stopped, and I looked. It was a crystal-like salt rock, and I was left wondering how many of these were actually sold each day versus how many just disappeared!

Crystal salt rock for sale

The next day, I decided to sleep in and go to the National Aquarium in the early afternoon. I still don't do a good job of building rest days into my schedule. I walked across the street from my hotel to the Aquarium at 2 PM. One of the things the museum operators pride themselves on is that all species in the aquarium are found in Namibian waters. I took some pictures of the fish there and then waited for the 3 PM feeding. The design, which has the visitor walking through a tunnel while the fish swim around you, is very clever. Among the fish were two species of stingrays which swam in their own pool. Three different species of sharks, one small and two larger ones, were in the main pool. Also in its own tank was a serpent eel. I took note of local lobsters that seemed to be much smaller than Bermudian lobsters. That reminded me that I hadn't eaten lobster yet on my trip. I would have to change that.

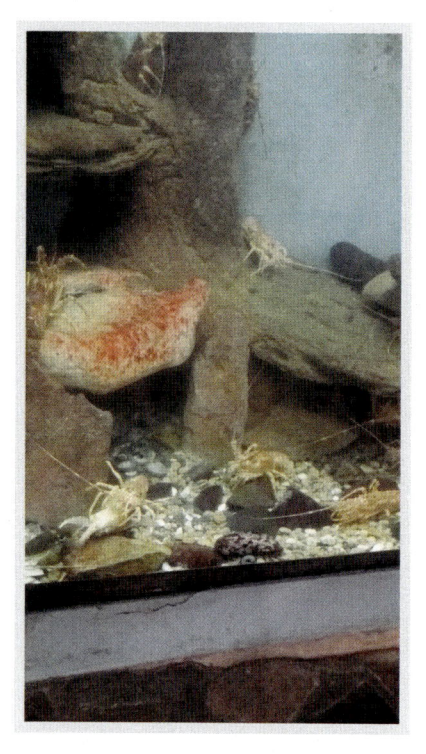

Lobsters at the national aquarium

I was expecting a feeding frenzy at 3 PM, but I guess if you know you're going to be fed every day there is no need to " jump the line" and try to eat everything that's thrown into the tank! In fact, what I noticed was that a fish would have a piece of food, bite some off and release the rest. As it was drifting to the bottom another fish would take it and do the same. This would continue until that piece was gone. I didn't see any fish (large or small) tearing pieces away from a fish who already had it. Maybe they were simply on their best behaviour.

On Friday, I was off to the Rossing uranium mine tour. I went to the pick-up spot in town and from there the Rossing bus took us 55 km back in the direction of Windhoek, a forty-five-minute drive in the countryside. This mine was opened in 1976, a decade after Rio Tinto, a mining company which operated in forty countries around the world, had secured the rights to operate this mine. It was a long time coming as uranium deposits were first discovered in 1928. This was one of the most productive mines in the world, as it provided 2.5% of the world's uranium oxide. Namibia is the fifth largest producer in the world and holds 7% of the world's reserves. The bulk of the output from this mine goes to China and France. Spot prices for uranium had been down for three years running but the company increased output to offset the price drop. The spot price for the end of January 15 was $37, January 16 $34.70, January 17 $24.50 and January 18 $21.88—serious price loss!

Uranium mine

Uranium mine

97% of the staff is Namibian with women making up 17% which must be a very high percentage for a field such as this. Most of the workers live in three nearby towns. Buses collect and return them at the end of their shifts. Because of this, there was no need for a large parking area.

Upon entry to the plant, employees must take a drug test. Any test failure results in that person being sent home until there is a hearing. Training in all areas is important to the company. There are a high number of staff who have been with the company for more than a decade and training plays a big part in this. The company was proud to point out that there had been two million work hours without an accident. This was certainly something to be proud of.

There was an open pit which has been in operation for over forty years. There are three shifts which maintain 24-hour daily operation. Shipments move in and out by train with drums of uranium oxide being sent to Walvis Bay for delivery overseas. All waste is kept on-site, as radiation is possible. Should the spot price rise, some of the waste may be reworked as it could be profitable at the higher price.

We drove through the site and could see cleanliness and safety concerns within the plant, including a pile of uranium. Additionally, looking at the open pit from the top again clearly showed the regard for safety. I was very impressed with the way the company's operations were carried out. I was able to look at the operation from the viewing point and could see how the pit had been cut over the years in a very safe way. And, like so many other things I didn't know before starting my research for this trip, I had no idea Namibia was in the uranium business!

Next, I wanted to go south to Walvis Bay. The next day I took a minivan for the forty-minute ride between the two cities. I don't think 'cities' is the correct term when you consider that Swakopmund has 63,000 people and Walvis Bay has 45,000 except that at these population levels, they are the second and third largest 'cities' in the country.

It was very windy as we drove along. One of the more interesting things we did was to look at the style and size of the houses as we left Swakopmund. I had a nice place to stay in Walvis Bay, not too far from the dunes. I was wondering where a name such as Walvis Bay came from, but the translation solved that. In the native language 'Walvis' means Whale. So, the name of Whale Bay reflected the many whales that passed in days gone by. Currently, there's a whale watching season which runs from June to November when migrating humpback whales stop to play and to mate. In addition, great white sharks can be found all along the Atlantic coastline.

On my first day in Walvis Bay, I decided to go out on a sailing boat in and around the harbour. The dock area was very busy as there were several boats taking tourists out on the water. I joined in with the many who were waiting to get on to a boat. Once my sailboat unloaded, we were allowed on. The first thing we found was that there were free riders—large sea gulls. To challenge us even more for space were the three seals that followed us during our trip and from time to time, when they wanted to relax, they'd climb onboard.

Seal onboard

It was a beautiful day. The sky was clear, and the sea wasn't too rough, unlike what I'd seen up the coast at Swakopmund. There were several vessels involved in the oil extraction business in the water ahead of us. Even more interesting were the oil Derrick that were anchored there as well. As we sailed, we went very close to these Derrick and what we saw was impressive. Walvis Bay is very industrial, so we saw some of the normal activity at the harbour.

Oil rig

The following day, I got up early and soon after daybreak I got a taxi to take me 11 km out of town to Dune 7. This was a tall dune which people climb sometimes as a test-run for the great Big Daddy dune in the desert. The driver commented on the strong winds, which he said had been blowing for two weeks. Apparently, these were unseasonal winds as they were so strong. I'd definitely seen the force of the wind when driving south from Swakopmund to Walvis Bay but I was hoping that by moving early I could be up and down before the wind really picked up.

Dune 7

Boy, was I wrong! When the driver dropped me off no one was around. Bad sign? I didn't yet know.

I walked over to the starting point. It's usually uncommon to go straight up the dune as opposed to working your way along the ridge. This takes longer, but it's easier on the body. I'd also been told it's better to go up in your socks as opposed to shoes or boots, so off went my shoes. Of course, since one is going to climb in socks, the start must be at dawn. This is because it gets terribly hot on the dunes as the day progresses and you would not like to be halfway up when the fire in your feet becomes unbearable.

I headed for the ridge believing I had a chance. I could see great amounts of sand being blown off the top of two nearby dunes, but the activity on Dune 7 was far less. So l set off. The initial part was easy. I was 10% of the way up. The next part was even easier as the wind had blown away a lot of loose sand and I was walking on solid ground.

So far, so good.

When I started again the wind picked up so badly, I was seriously concerned about being blown over. Having made some further headway, I stopped and waited only to feel the wind getting stronger. At this point safety had to take precedence and I turned and worked my way back to the ground; however, before reaching the bottom, a tourist couple started the climb, taking the same route I had. We snapped a few pictures of each other then I went down and watched their effort. They started strong, but the challenge of the wind got the better of them and they turned back before getting as far as I did. Once down they quickly left.

While I sat waiting for my driver to return, another couple came. They tackled the dune head-on, going straight up the center. Maybe that was the best windy day tactic as they continued higher and higher until they were about 85% of the way to the top. Unfortunately, they too were forced back down. By the time I left, the weather was winning 3-0., but there was nothing to be ashamed of. Dune 7 is the eighth largest in the world at 388 m and it's situated between the Namib Desert and the Atlantic Ocean, which guarantees that most days will be a tough day for a climb.

After a bit of rest and relaxation, I went back to the waterfront to see the flamingos. Upon leaving the apartment, I walked past a cricket ground. It turned out to be the ICC Academy ground where Bermuda played Namibia in an ICC cricket match that Bermuda lost. Sadly, my visit to the harbour turned out to be a rare case of overpromote and under deliver. I'd read reviews and comments about a large flock of flamingos at the waterfront and how beautiful they were. When I got there, I was unimpressed with the size of the flock, but worse still, they were not close to the shore and they were so far away, I was unable to really see them. I believe I could have passed on this little excursion. The compensation was having a pleasant dinner at the Raft over the water.

The Raft

    This restaurant was said to be one of the best on the Namibian coast. It's built on stilts on its own jetty. Featuring seafood, there was a great atmosphere along with great views of the Walvis Bay lagoon. I thoroughly enjoyed my fish dinner as the sunset came in. I would recommend this restaurant in a flash as the location and atmosphere are great, the staff are amazing, and most importantly, the food is excellent.

Chapter 7
Journeying to Lüderitz and the Desert

"Take only memories, leave only footprints."
~Chief Seattle,1780-1866—Suquamish chief~

I left my hotel in Walvis Bay at 8:30 AM, after having breakfast to sustain myself. A taxi took me to the depot area where I got in a car that would take me to Windhoek over the next four hours. The car had one seat left, so once I got in it headed out. I've been impressed by the homes, commercial buildings, and general cleanliness of this country, so I'd been wondering if this was how everyone lived. As the car left the depot, we passed a section of town that wasn't as nice as others I'd seen previously. I took two pictures to try and provide some balance. This four-hour journey was provided at a cost of USD $12—not too bad at all. Again, I enjoyed the countryside as I went back to the capital city driving on nicely paved roads.

Once I got to the end of the journey, I had to get a local taxi to take me to the crosstown depot for minivans going south to Keetmanshoop. That was my destination for the day. Arriving at approximately 1 PM, I found that the next minivan heading out had two seats left after I got in. We sat waiting for the next people to arrive, which happened at about 2:30 PM.

This felt like West Africa!

Keetmanshoop was to be a five-hour journey; however, we made a stop along the way that was a bit long. After about four hours, the nicely paved road turned into a gravel road which was full of bumps. I didn't arrive in Keetmanshoop until 8 PM. To be honest, I was a bit worried as the night wore on since the research I'd done warned against night-driving, due to both driver recklessness and animals wandering across the highway. I knew first-hand about the animal part from my experience in Gabon when the young elephant was killed by the train. Additionally, the driver's recklessness was evidenced by the number of crosses along the roadside, bearing testament to the impact of careless driving.

I arrived in the dark and there was no sign of taxis. Fortunately, my hotel, Schützenhaus Guest House, was only 800 m from where I was standing, so I walked to the hotel. It was an old German-style building which had been built in 1907 and was now operated by a German. This place was the oldest German club in southern Namibia. It had a nice setting with many historic accents, some of which clearly aren't politically correct, but that's not my battle. I should point out that Keetmanshoop is a stopover and not a destination. It took me twelve hours, door to door, to complete my journey because I really wanted to go to a place called Lüderitz at the very south of the country. It's on the Atlantic coast, so with a good road one could have run straight down the coast from Walvis Bay in maybe four hours. Instead, I had to take the long journey route. Going right through to Lüderitz may have taken until midnight and I didn't think it would be wise to arrive at that time, so I stopped in Keetmanshoop.

The next day, rather than getting the first thing smoking out of town and punishing my body with more grueling time in a van, I stayed in town and toured the two points of interest. There was a species of trees named Quiver trees that are as old as 200 years in the area. Additionally, there are large rocks stacked upon each other like a small child's building blocks. This second area has been given the name of Giant's Playground. I walked into town and tried to get a taxi to take me 13 km to see the trees. The Giant's Playground is a further 5 km on the same road, so I figured I would ask to be taken there once we got to the first spot.

Surprise for me—the taxis didn't want to go there. Now think about it: only two points of interest, close to each other, and the taxis don't want to go? So, I walked to the tourist bureau where neither of the two people in the office seemed interested in talking with me. Once the more senior of the two was identified, I asked how I could get there, but he didn't know. Finally, he suggested I walk over to a nearby hotel and inquire, but by that time my body temperature was rising. Instead of blowing my top I left and proceeded to the place he'd recommended.

The lady at the hotel suggested I call a man who had a flier in her office for renting cars. I called and having explained the problem, he said he'd take me himself in fifteen minutes for a very reasonable fee. As l like to say," what was that all about." Fifteen minutes later, the man (a police officer in uniform) appeared, telling me it was his lunch break. So, off we went. We visited four different locations to take pictures and at no point did he appear to be in any hurry to return to his police duties. He'd temporarily transitioned into the tourism business.

STORY OF THE QUIVER TREES

The quiver tree is found in the hot, dry deserts of Namibia and northern South Africa. It got the name because some of the San people used the tough bark and branches to make quivers on their arrows. The quiver tree grows up to 30 ft. They usually grow singly but sometimes grow together, giving the look of a forest in the desert. This was what I saw during my tour as this forest is one of the few spontaneous quiver tree forests. It's estimated that there are about 250 trees in this area. One interesting aspect of the trees is that they look like they're growing upside down, with the branches that look like roots. They have a bright yellow flower which grows only in the winter months of June and July, though I didn't see any., as none have been planted by man, but they continue to survive by Quiver trees grow among black rock formations that absorb the summer heat, usually 100F. Apparently, these trees are natural to the forest the spread of seeds. This forest was declared a national monument by the government in 1995.

Quiver trees

As I mentioned, Giant's Playground is given this name because of the way the huge dolerite rocks have been placed upon one another. These placements create many strange rock formations, some as high as three-story buildings. When you look at the area, it appears as if giant-sized children must have thrown these rocks around aimlessly.

Giant's Playground

After the hassle back in town, I was very grateful to the police officer who made this little stopover quite delightful. He took on the role of tour guide and gave me excellent explanations of both the sites and some background to the town.

Once I was dropped back into the town, I walked around a bit looking at its historic aspects before returning to my lodgings. Both nights, I had dinner at the guesthouse and ate from a German menu. The second night there was a World Cup match of some interest to those living in the town, so they had booked the dining room for an authentic German meal. After eating, they enjoyed the match. I found it interesting to watch the interaction of those attending.

Another travel day. I left the hotel, walked to the nearby depot, and arrived there at 9:30 AM; but the van didn't leave until almost 12 PM.

Now, this feels like Bo, Sierra Leone.

I was going from my stop off point of Keetmanshoop to the south of the country to an oceanside town named Lüderitz. The trip should have taken five hours, but with the late start I'd only have time to check in at the hotel and go for dinner. I'd be quite disappointed if it turned out that way. At least I'd have lots of legroom.

This country has a lot of open space. In contrast to Bermuda, where we are said to be the eleventh most densely populated country in the world, Namibia is the third *least* densely populated country in the world. On this day, once again, we were driving through the Namib Naukluft National Park desert, which is said to be both the world's oldest and driest desert. This is the second largest desert in the world behind only the Sahara. The landscape was beautiful, though I'm sure it's a challenge to drive for hours in the desert. Occasionally we passed small flocks of sheep, but I saw nothing else that looked to be alive.

Driving in the desert

As we got closer to Lüderitz the wind grew stronger. It blew sand across the road and even pushed the van from side to side a couple of times. What surprised me was that when we were 5 km from our destination, we were still in the desert with sand dunes nearby. Soon after, large, black volcanic rocks became the surface possibly because all the top surface had been blown away over time.

We entered Lüderitz through the "working class" part of town. I took a few pictures of the housing there.

Housing for the working class

Getting a cab, it didn't take too long to get across town to my apartment. Even in this small town I, who'd never been here in my life, had to give the driver directions. As is so often the case, showing him *maps.me* didn't solve the problem or enlighten him in any way. I'd been warned by my readings that this would be the cold part of my journey and it was. The wind coming off the Atlantic was frigid.

There was hardly any grass in Lüderitz giving it a very barren look. Because it was a German colonial town only dating back to 1908 when the Germans arrived searching for diamonds, this led to Lüderitz being the first German colony in Africa.

My short stay was a step back in time as much of the town remains as it was when the Germans were expelled in 1914. Lüderitz is still a small town, having a population of 12,000 people. It has a wild coast due to the wind and rain and has interesting sea life. One can finds seals, penguins, flamingos as well as previously mentioned, whales and great white sharks. This is an important fishing area as well. While walking through the town one afternoon I went into a fish distribution place where individuals can have fish shipped to them in the major urban areas. In fact, people take public transport from as far away as Windhoek to buy to order for friends or their own small group of customers.

I went to dinner at one of the best restaurants in Lüderitz called Barrels Restaurant and Bar. They had a delicious buffet meal, which had a variety of seafood along with some beef items as well. The restaurant was set up like an old cave tavern, which was very much in keeping with the old town itself. I walked to the restaurant but when I came out the wind was so strong, I couldn't possibly walk back. I stood in a place protected from the wind where I was able to see passing traffic. After a while, I got a cab with a very friendly driver. Seeing the wisdom of having a reliable driver, I asked if he could take me where I needed to go while I was in town. He agreed and put an end to my transportation issue in this location. The next morning, my prearranged driver picked me up and drove 10 km from Lüderitz to a ghost town named Kolmanskop. Along the way, I was looking out for wild horses said to be about halfway between the two places, but to my disappointment, I didn't see any.

This town was created when there was a diamond rush in the very early part of the twentieth century. In 1880, a German businessman named Arthur Luderitz purchased the land which became the town known by his name for £200 plus 200 rifles from the local Namib chief. He believed copper could be found there but turned out it couldn't, and he missed the diamonds because he was determined to find the copper! Diamonds were found thirty years later and in the early days of the diamond rush, men went out in the early evening and simply picked up rocks that glinted in the light. Diamonds remain important to the country's economy today as Namibia is the eighth largest producer in the world.

A town which was given the name Kolmanskop started in 1908 with German prospectors looking to get rich. Many diamonds were found, including some very big ones.

Diamond examples

At one point, Kolmanskop was called the richest little town in the world. The first houses were built in 1908 and the town was electrified by 1911. Imagine that! There was a 250-bed hospital (there are many communities today throughout the world that don't have 250 bed hospitals) and it had an x-ray machine. Of course, the x-ray machine had a dual purpose. It was used to x-ray the sick and the diamond thieves. The head doctor believed that a glass of wine helped to improve one's health, so every patient was given a glass every morning. I wonder how many tried to get into the hospital for the wine…

At its peak there were three hundred adults plus children and eight hundred native workers who were brought from the north of the country to work there. There were many advanced technologies and luxuries that a rich little town could afford. For instance, every house had a freezer box, and every house received half a block of ice daily from the icehouse at no cost. Rather than settling for bush meat, meat was brought in from Keetmanshoop, five hours up the road. They got cattle and pigs which allowed them to enjoy a normal German diet while living miles from Germany. The town became an oasis of German culture in the desert! Even there in the desert, distinction was made between the important folks and the rest. There was a row of houses called Millionaires Row. The important people in the town were assigned these residences. The mine engineer, the quartermaster, the accountant, and the school principal were some of those who lived in this prestigious area.

A 1908 house built in the middle of nowhere

Unfortunately, diamonds were found a short way to the south in the late 1920s. This impacted the attractiveness of this site with the result being that the last building built there was in 1925. By 1938 all production ceased at Kolmanskop and the men went to the nearest profitable site while the children and women remained; but in 1958 this was no longer deemed viable, and people moved away leaving the town to decay. Each year, more sand is driven inside the remaining buildings by the strong winds.

Sand accumulating inside this house

In the 1970s, consideration was given to opening the town as a tourist attraction, but this didn't happen until 1990. It gets around 35,000 annual visitors who are moving south to north in their tour of Namibia. There are warnings about some unsafe buildings and the tour guide caution against hyenas and deadly snakes such as the puffer adder.

Saturday—another travel day. I covered 500 km from Lüderitz to Windhoek on good roads all the way. Needing to get to the "leave when full" van early, I was up at 7 AM, and on my way shortly thereafter. I had to wait almost ninety minutes for the van to leave. Finally, at around 9 AM, we were racing along the two-lane highway. In this area you can drive for long periods without passing another vehicle. It really isn't a place to hitchhike, and I'd feel sorry for anyone who had car problems. I had read of young tourists standing by the road for up to four hours trying to catch a ride. It's not a good idea, especially when you consider the weather conditions.

We were driving through the desert once again with its marvellous rock formations and sand dunes. Not having to drive, it's very pleasant to watch the scenery go by. The van was quiet. Having left early, most were probably tired, so they were asleep, and the driver didn't play any music. I was thankful for this as the music is almost always played with the bass leading an assault on my ears.

At 12:30 PM, we made a half-hour stop at Keetmanshoop. Three people got off and luckily, the driver was able to get three new travelers. We'd been doing well timewise, as it only took three and a half hours to get to Keetmanshoop. Now on to Windhoek!

About half an hour later, we saw a pick-up truck turned upside down on the side of the road. It seemed as if the accident had occurred only a short while earlier, but there was no sign of anyone injured. Once more I was pleased to not be driving on what could easily have been called a long and boring road.

We continued without incident. Upon reaching Windhoek, I got a taxi to my new hotel which was located one block from the CBD.

CBD?

When I first heard this term, I had no idea what the person was talking about. Later, I found out it was short for Central Business District. I was happy with the location and the hotel itself. I was also glad to be back in the city in time to see the World Cup final, which I watched the following day at a bar. France was just too strong for Croatia. This was possibly my second rest-day of the trip, coming at the end of the seventh week.

I went to get supplies for my trip into the desert. I was concerned about how cold it would be at night, so I bought a jacket to wear. I caught a big sale and was able to get a good quality product at a reasonable price.

Next, I walked over to Parliament to sit in the gallery and see the proceedings in action. I'd seen the parliamentary calendar online, so I knew the House would be sitting today as it was due to meet four times each week during July. I'd also learnt that in the last parliamentary session the House failed to meet eleven times due to lack of a quorum. I was unimpressed by this because the government had such a majority in the House that if all the Opposition members boycotted the business of the House it would still go on. The government has seventy-seven of the ninety-six seats, with the fifteen opposition parties having only nineteen seats. Clearly it was the failure of the Government Whip to keep government members in line that led to a lack of quorum. This gave me cause to question the government's commitment to good governance.

When I arrived at the entrance of the House, I was told the House had risen for the summer—twelve sittings early! I was completely unimpressed. So much for good governance.

MY TRIP INTO THE DESERT

I was picked up at 8 AM, after a large breakfast and storing my bag at the hotel. I planned to return after the tour, so there was no need to take all my stuff. I also had to buy a recharger for my phone. Otherwise, I'd have no contact for three days. The cost was N$40 for a week or service. Imagine, USD $3.

The tour group included eight people with Japanese, Americans and me in a comfortable van. As an aside, there was an American of Indian, as in India, heritage who was wearing dreadlocks. As it turned out, he was a schoolteacher who'd just completed two years in Rwanda and was going back to the States after he completed three months of touring. I was impressed by his dreads, which had been sown into his head.

We drove back on the road that I travelled on from Lüderitz for an hour. Then we took a road into the desert. The scenery was great. We passed mountains, scrublands, and trees. I also saw two shooting ranges, a flock of sheep and horses and donkeys for trail rides.

At 1 PM-ish, we stopped at a beautiful lookout known as Spreetshoogte Pass and had lunch on the road. This was a team effort as dividing up the task made it easier to get going again. Soon after we started, the driver stopped and got a king cricket from the side of the road. Don't ask me how he spotted the cricket. As it turned out, some tribes are these. Happy eating!

We'd been travelling about 1500m above sea level but now we began our descent. Beautiful scenes abound. Our next stop was a wayside village called Solitaire, for their famous apple strudel at the Moose McGregor bakery. This is one of those places that thrive because of frequent mentions in guidebooks. Nevertheless, the apple strudel was very good with hot chocolate—definitely worth stopping for. It's funny, but some people give this food a poor rating, but I believe it's because they think it's pie and are disappointed. I should also mention that the only gas station for miles around is at this stop.

Moose McGregor famous apple strudel

We travelled on to our campsite at Sossusvlei. There were many other groups there, as this is one of Namibia's most popular tourism spots. We left our camping gear and immediately drove to Elim Dune. This is a medium size dune which we all climbed before sunset and took many amazing pictures. I was almost overwhelmed by the beauty of the desert. Once the sun went down the tour groups marched off the dune like a little army. This was a "welcome to climbing the big dunes" warm up! Leaving the dune, we saw two Oryx standing under the trees nearby.

Back at the campsite while dinner was cooking, mattresses and sleeping bags were sorted out. I'm not a camper by any stretch of the imagination, having gone to Allen camp on Port's Island one summer when I was about twelve years old, so this is close to a new experience for me. I even helped to erect a couple of the tents and learnt that if properly done, it's not so hard at all! Stop laughing, you veteran campers!

Get that tent up, young man

Dinner was very average (to be polite) and after chatting for a while, we turned in. I'd been concerned about how cold it would be, thus the new jacket; but to my surprise, it was hot in the tent and, having started with layers, I ended up in a T-shirt and shorts. I hadn't expected this outcome.

Day Two in the desert.

Our first task was to get ready. We were told the night before that we would leave camp in the dark at 6:30 AM to drive forty-five minutes to Dune 45, one of the largest of the dunes, to see the sunrise from the top of the dune. So, at 6:35 AM, we were driving through the gates of the camp and heading for the dunes. It was a very quiet ride as, not being able to see anything, most probably went back to sleep. When we arrived, we joined other groups that were scrambling up the dune. Yes, this big one looked fearsome! I started up and at first all was well, but as I went further along, I became challenged. Despite this, I continued on... and on. I passed people who were sitting in the sand content to see the sunrise from their spot and unwilling to go any further. Finally, after much huffing and puffing, I reached the top. I was able to get some lovely pictures from that vantage point and had the satisfaction of climbing this big dune which is 80m high. Of course, I was busted but personal determination had kept me going that morning, as it has on many others since I started these travels in fall 2014.

Now it was breakfast time. The driver/guide/cook had set out a rather simple breakfast and, after eating, we headed off for Deadvlei and Big Daddy. Big Daddy is the largest of the dunes and Deadvlei is the site of the 600 year-old camelthorn trees.

The drive to this site is about 45 km. When we got there our vehicle became unusable as it got stuck in reverse gear. This created a crisis as we still had to go 4 km to get to the dunes; and of course, we had to go back to our campsite. Alternative arrangements had to be made, which included sending another vehicle out of Windhoek. As a result, we took a shuttle to the dunes. Having successfully climbed two in the last twelve hours, I decided not to take Big Daddy and walked through the heavy sand to Deadvlei. It was quite a sight.

By the way, Big Daddy is so named because it is 325 m (or 1066 ft.) Common sense kicked in as I knew Big Daddy was a bit too challenging for me after trekking the two previous ones. I was happy to stand in its shadow.

Big Daddy

    Deadvlei is a white clay pan. The land is covered with a layer of salt and clay. The camelthorn trees, a dense hardwood, grew many years ago when the Tsauchab river flooded this area. Once the rains stopped the trees died. The wood doesn't decompose as it simply is too dry. The trees are a protected species and must not be damaged by people. This is a bizarre yet beautiful place. These trees can be found in South Africa, Botswana, and Zimbabwe in addition to Namibia.

Camelthorn trees

After a bit of a wait, we were taken back to the campsite in another company's vehicle. The only problem with this was that it had open sides and was to be driven at 20 km per hour (the fastest it could go under the circumstances) instead of 80 km per hour. Everyone grabbed something to cover their face as the wind and sand pummeled us. After what seemed like a lifetime, we got back to the camp. While we were covering our faces, the driver managed to see an ostrich and some springboks on the side of the road. He said he was stopping to allow some picture taking, but I really believed he had a kind heart and stopped to give us a rest from the sand-beating we were getting.

We had a visit to Sesriem Canyon as our last scheduled activity for the day. We had no vehicle but over lunch the driver explained that the canyon was a forty-five-minute walk away and the group decided to do so. Brave bunch! We rested for an hour and then walked to the canyon. The driver hadn't been lying about the time required for the walk. It took us fifty minutes. The canyon was a sight to behold. Over the many years, the Tsauchab River, which does not exist most years, has worked its way through the canyon and deepened it. This has been going on for over two million years.

It last rained here in 2008. The canyon is about 1 km long and at its deepest, 30 m or 100 ft.

A visit to Sesriem Canyon

We walked the length of the canyon which, while being quite wide in some places, was very narrow in others, requiring a squeeze to get through. The best time to view the colours is at sunrise or sunset. We stayed at the canyon until sunset, which allowed us to see the beautiful rock formations. Then we managed to get rides with two other tour groups back to our campsite. I was glad we didn't miss this opportunity.

It had been another beautiful day in the desert.

It was time to return to Windhoek. Given the distance, Day Three of this trip was simply a desert drive. To make the day interesting, the trip back was on another route. The highlight was to be a stop at the Tropic of Capricorn sign. Still tired, we were up at 8 AM for breakfast. The company had sent another vehicle, though it turned out that it wasn't as sturdy as the previous one and we were going to have a bumpy ride.

Two other men from the company were present, one of whom had driven the replacement vehicle. However, the pack-up exercise fell on our driver/ guide and the eight tourists while these two watched until the very end. As a result, things lagged, and we didn't leave until 10 AM. Every now and again, there are insubordinate staff who ruin the experience for the very people who pay their salaries. I guess this happens everywhere in the world.

We drove to Solitaire, where we'd stopped on the way down and got gas and snacks. Soon after getting back on the road, we came upon an accident. A tour vehicle was lying across the road, overturned. There must have been twelve to fifteen people in the vehicle including five children. Fortunately, only two women had suffered minor injuries while another lady had broken a leg as well as having pains in her neck. These travelers were very fortunate that they hadn't suffered worse. Our drivers stopped and helped.

Overturned vehicle

As I mentioned, before leaving our campsite, we'd secured promises from the two drivers that we'd travel the route that led to the Tropic of Capricorn. Sure enough, we stopped at the sign and took pictures.

Tropic of Capricorn signage

The Tropic of Capricorn is the southernmost latitude where the sun can be directly overhead and runs parallel to the equator. It's also the dividing line between the southern temperate zone to the south and the tropics to the north. From that point on it was a quiet and safe drive back to the city. My second desert experience was over and had been very eventful.

Chapter 8
Journeying to Lüderitz and the Desert

"There are no foreign lands. It is the traveller only who is foreign."
~Robert Louis Stevenson, 1850-1894—Scottish novelist, poet, and travel writer~

I took another rest day. Other than looking for some gifts from the Namibia craft center, I didn't do much at all. I wanted to rest after the desert trip and before the trip to the game park. I had two interesting exchanges at the craft center. First, much of the crafts are made by the Himba tribe and sold in the markets by the Himba women. This is a little tricky as when I was talking with the vendor and making my purchase, I had to keep saying to myself, "Direct eye contact only!"

For those readers who are not aware of why I had to do this, look up *the Himba Tribe of Namibia* on the Internet and you'll understand.

Secondly, one of the other vendors asked if I was Theo-Ben Gurirab's brother. Of course, I had no idea who Theo-Ben Gurirab was. The man explained that Mr. Gurirab was one of Namibia's political heroes. He was the second Prime Minister of the new independent nation and later served as Speaker of the House for ten years. He'd died the previous year. Later, looking at his picture, I could see a resemblance!

I had dinner at a very nice restaurant which sells in large quantities, so having ordered a steak and prawns, the prawns were huge, and the steak covered the plate! This restaurant was on the edge of the city on a hill overlooking an area going far into the distance. The waiter explained that all the eye could see was a large ghetto. People had come to the city seeking opportunities and their starting point was almost always this place. This was one of the burning issues in the country as the SWAPO government had promised land to the people upon taking over the running of the country but not too much progress had been made in this regard.

The next morning the safari company picked me up at 7 AM and started the journey north. It was a six-hour journey of 380 miles with plenty of good scenery. I was touring with the same company and the same guide that had taken me into the desert a few days ago. We travelled on a nicely tarred road the entire way and drove three hours to a small town where we stopped for supplies. We then carried on to the town of Oujo where we gassed up. This last stop was less than 60 miles to Etosha National Park. Most of the drive had been in highly urban areas.

When we reached the main gate, we still had a 15 km drive to our camp. During this drive we saw zebras, ostriches, giraffes, and springbok. It was exciting and we weren't even at the camp yet! We drove into the camp and found it to be a large campsite. We didn't have to set up our tents, so I went to the waterhole nearby to see which animals would come for water midday. I happily watched as elephants came to drink. Why was I happy? I was in my twelfth country in this series of trips to Africa and I was finally in a quality game park.

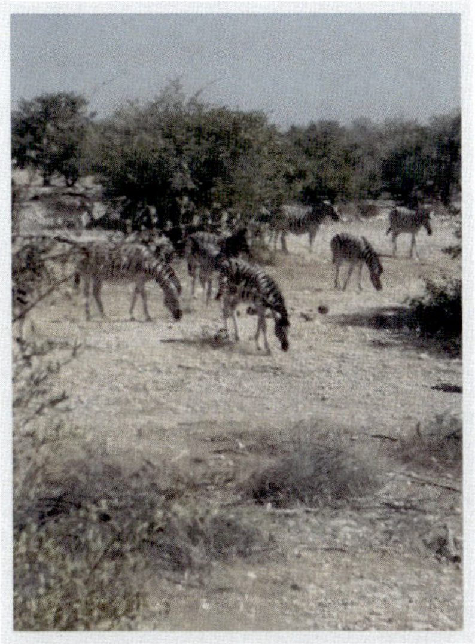

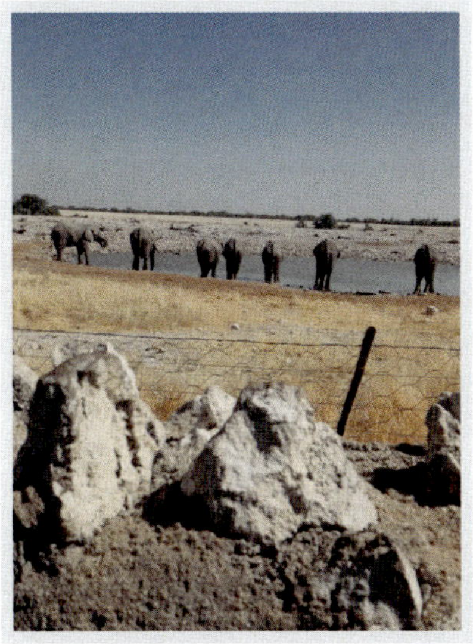

After having some food, we set out on our first game drive at 3 PM. We saw three elephants, giraffes, ground squirrels, oryx (a large antelope) and springing springboks, as well as black jacket jackals. I say *springing* springboks as the springbok gets its name from jumping or springing to get away quickly when it chooses to, and we saw one do just that. It seemed that the springbok were the most numerous of the animals in the park.

The game drive ended at around 6 PM, and we were free until dinner, which was to be at approximately 8 PM. I headed back to the waterhole. While there I only saw elephants but what a sight as they paraded in walking in single file, taking control of the waterhole.

We had a lovely campfire dinner and after this I headed for the waterhole again. This time I saw three elephants and six giraffes. One of the guides explained that giraffes are not preyed upon in the wild because they use a very powerful kick to defend themselves. The final highlight of the day was seeing two rhinoceros coming out of the shadows and entering the waterhole. What a sight!

Rhinos at the waterhole

And this was just Day One!

For me, our first night in the game park was marred by some gentlemen who were sitting up talking at 5 AM. I wanted to sleep, not listening to them. They weren't part of my group, so I really couldn't go and sort them out. To add to this, someone's car started to honk about half an hour later. This went on for about ten minutes then thankfully stopped… only to start again about ten minutes later. Ugh.

We were all up and eager to see the animals at 7 AM. We had a quick cup of coffee and biscuit before leaving for our first morning game drive when the gate opened at 7:30 AM. We all had one of our blankets wrapped around us, as it was very cold in the morning. Remember, it was winter, so we had to do this every morning.

Once we were on the move, there were plenty of springboks to see. At our first waterhole stop we were excited to see both a lion and lioness. It was funny to see how the springbok gave them space while keeping a careful eye on them. Lions eat every three or four days. If they have recently eaten, they won't kill for sport. We were hoping to see the lions in action, but this was not to be, so we moved to a second waterhole. Here we saw many zebras and a few oryx.

Lion in our pathway

Elephants in our pathway

Giraffes in our pathway

At 10 AM, we returned to our camp. In contrast to the night before, there were fewer tents which meant many others had finished their trips to the national park and left. Hence, it was a quiet camp. We had a morning brunch of tasty breakfast food before having a break. Some went to bed in their tents while others walked around the camp to get their bearings. I did the same thing I did whenever we had a break—went to the camp waterhole. It was now around noon, and it was so interesting to watch as the different animal species used the waterhole in an almost orderly fashion. As always there were many springboks. They'd dart into the water and drink in between the other animals taking turns. This time the wildebeest came and drank. When they were finished the zebras came but drank very quickly and were soon out of the hole. As they left, the springboks took over the waterhole once more.

At 2 PM, we started out for an afternoon drive. At our first waterhole stop we saw a lion, springbok, ostrich, zebra and a few oryx. Later, as we moved around, we saw impalas with their black faces and four male kudos. Only the males have antlers. Before the drive was over, we saw three prides of elephants and two rhinos.

This was interesting because we could sit safely in our vehicle and got quite close to the animals at times.

Our second day in the game park arrived. Again, we got up early, had our coffee and biscuits and were out the gate at 7:30 AM. During our morning drive we had the excitement of seeing two lions and one lioness. During the remainder of the morning drive, we didn't see any other animals (apart from springbok) so we returned to camp for our morning brunch. When asked, our guide was unable to say why the game would be so scarce that morning.

After eating, I went to the camp waterhole where I saw zebras and three babies. The babies had an all-black coat. By the time they are nine months old, their cover will be the black and white stripes one expects to see on a zebra. I then watched the march as the zebras were followed by kudos, which were followed by wildebeest, elephants and lastly, oryx. I got a big chuckle watching these animals behaving in such an orderly manner.

Our afternoon drive found ostriches, giraffes and elephants going through the forest. I was able to get video footage of the elephants. We saw more giraffes at a waterhole stop. Then we saw elephants in the bush as well as the animals we'd seen on the afternoon drive, but even more exciting was when our driver spotted a lion hiding in the grass. We were somewhat disappointed because the lion was eating and obviously, we'd missed the kill.

At that point I need to praise the guide. Some years ago, I went to Kruger National Park in South Africa. It's still regarded as one of the premier game parks. Each vehicle had a radio and when one driver spotted a kill, he'd radio it out and your driver would join others, dashing to the location. Etosha doesn't have such a system. Instead, the driver relies on his knowledge of the park and the animal movements. Of course, when a driver finds something interesting it's verbally passed on. However, our driver often was the one making the find and sharing it with others. He'd been working in this park for five years and his skill could not be questioned.

Once again after dinner I went for a nighttime visit to the camp waterhole. I was not to be disappointed as I saw elephants and two black rhinos. I should point out that the black rhinos are now classified as endangered, so seeing them at the waterhole was a real treat. The endangered status is mainly due to the severe increase in poaching. These animals are poached for their horns, which are used in traditional Asian medicine. The horns are ground into a fine powder and used as treatment for a variety of illnesses.

Rhino

The following day was my last morning to enjoy the wildlife at Etosha National Park. We'd been fortunate to have seen most of the larger species during our tour. Only the nocturnal leopard and the evasive cheetah remained unseen. We had another early breakfast at 7 AM. The gates were opened at 7:30 AM, and out we went in search of the leopard and cheetah. We'd barely started when we turned into the very first waterhole and saw four lionesses lying in pairs. Great start, lots of pictures taken.

We then seriously went after the two elusive animals, but with no success. Our game drive did find two young elephants that were having a battle of strength until the one that appeared to be losing then turned its attention to us and proceeded to follow us. Of course, he was moving at a somewhat slower pace than our vehicle. I think he was being clever and used our presence to avoid a beating.

As we drove from place to place searching, we came upon a group of zebras including three very pregnant ones. The gestation period for these African zebras is believed to be thirteen months. Finally, our time was up, and we drove back to our campsite, thus ending our sixth game drive. Before going back to the city, we were to enjoy a late morning brunch. So, I went to the camp waterhole and made a video of the activity I saw. On the video I captured the ever-present springbok, a few kudos and a small number of zebras moving away. I also made a video of the camp to give an idea of the facility where I'd spent the last four days.

After our final meal, it was back to Windhoek. We arrived well after 5 PM, so the day was pretty much spent. Besides, after four days in the game park and three in the desert I was exhausted. For the next day (my last in Namibia), the plan was to do as little as possible. Of course, that was not to be the case. Instead, the next day I went around the city for a final look. I took pictures of the clock tower and the genocide monument. The clock tower is located on Independence Ave in the heart of the city. It's a replica of the original, which had been built in 1908. The genocide monument is a few feet from the Independence Museum. I took two pictures hoping that the inspiring words on the monument would be remembered. The words were: *Their blood waters our freedom.*

Brilliant.

Genocide monument

I finally started my journey back to my home, Bermuda. As I headed for my SAA flight, I saw the Namibian hills for the last time. Windhoek, to Joburg, to New York overnight and, lastly, LF Wade International Airport Bermuda, just in time for the final Cup Match trial.

Go Somerset!

Conclusion

This trip was very much a learning experience. When I started researching I knew very little about these countries but by the end I'd earned the right to say I'd seen how those countries which are "under the radar" can operate. My negative belief about long-term leaders was met by two, one of whom seemed to be holding his country back, while in the other country there were indications forward momentum. I was disappointed by the corruption that exists in some of these countries but was impressed by the average citizen's positive approach to life.

Poverty still exists and is a threat to the wellbeing of the people; however, none of these countries can be regarded as being in a hopeless state. All have resources that are valuable, and with effective management, they will do well for their people. In particular, the recent find of offshore oil in Namibian waters could prove to be a game changer. Health concerns must be addressed to ensure that life expectancy is increased and as education standards continue to rise, job opportunities must be created. Otherwise, there will be a brain drain to other countries offering the opportunities the young people seek.

For tourists, all three countries can ensure a great holiday with an opportunity to learn as well as play.

ABOUT THE AUTHOR

I am a traveller and a writer; however, I had a real life and a proper job before. I was a partner at Deloitte, a Minister in the Government of Bermuda and the owner of a real estate firm. When I retired in 2014, I became what I always wanted to be—a solo traveller. I had been to forty-eight countries but until Covid arrived, I went to 50 more, spending between one and six weeks in each country while travelling in eight week sequences away then home then away again. It has been quite the journey! My first two books, Immersed in West Africa, and A New Day Dawns, tell the tales of two trips of eight adventure-filled weeks in nine West African countries. Since then, I've been to thirteen additional African nations.

In my spare time, I love to read (especially researching future trips) and watch sports while spending time with my family.

REVIEW REQUEST

Thank you for taking time to read Let's Go to Gabon, Cameroon, and Namibia. If you enjoyed this book, please consider telling your friends and posting a review on Amazon. However, keep in mind that word of mouth is the author's best friend and so your positive comments are much appreciated.

A NEW DAY DAWNS

He was willing to let foreign cultures collide with his own perceptions. This time, they exceeded every expectation.

Terry Lister still wasn't done unearthing new experiences. After his harrowing travels through parts of West Africa, he set his sights on four more of the vast continent's countries in the hope of gleaning insights into unfamiliar values and intriguing local customs. And with the infamous Ivory Coast on his list-to-visit, he knew he'd be in for the unexpected.

Armed as usual with his meticulous research, Terry was prepared to venture far beyond tourist traps in his thirst for knowledge. But as he quickly realized, sometimes the most well-planned journeys reveal their deepest secrets when spontaneity strikes.

In this second installment, Terry Lister returns with his trademark wit and wisdom to share with readers his quest to show the side of a landscape rarely seen. And as he debunks the myths about danger and risk, heads to pristine beaches, and discovers ancient castles, this down-to-earth explorer delivers on his promise: an unforgettable adventure that will spark your soul.

A New Day Dawns: My Solo Journey Into West Africa is the hugely entertaining second book in the Travels with Terry travelogue series. If you like real-life stories, people who adore pushing boundaries, and spirited tales of solitary encounters, then you'll love this exciting dive into an incredible challenge.

Buy A New Day Dawns to see the sunrise with different eyes today.

EXCERPT

After more than a week in Freetown, it was time to move on and go to the countryside. In planning this trip, I decided to go to Bo, a major inland city in the southeastern part of the country. It is also the second largest city in the country and is a key place for the diamond industry.

The uncontrolled development of Freetown leaves both the airport and car transport far, far away. It took two hours to drive from my hotel to the car dispatch across town in normal traffic. Once there, I asked for the car to Bo. The car was almost full, and I was the one to fill it. So off we went – seven live bodies in a space meant for five.

The straight-line distance between the two cities is 108 miles. The driving distance is 147 miles or 36 miles per hour, which meant the journey should have taken approximately four hours. Not wishing to use up my phone battery and arrive with a phone that did not work, I did not check our progress until we had been on a very good road for three hours. At that point, I checked where we were on *maps.me*, and it was clear that the car was not going to Bo! Instead, the car was destined for another city in the middle of the country. I spoke with the driver who admitted his mistake in telling me he was going to Bo, but there was no recovery plan. I simply was unable to get to Bo that day.

Instead of leaving me to fend for myself, he drove to a guesthouse and tried to secure a room for me while I sat in the car. The price for a room was outrageous, as agreed by the other passengers still in the car, so, I turned it down, with their approval. The driver made some additional calls and took me to another guest house, where a far better price was offered and accepted by the other passengers! Meanwhile, these folks were being held up from continuing to their own destinations while I was being sorted out. Nice folks!

As a result, I had to spend the night there before heading off to Bo in the morning. This is what happened: I asked a simple question and got a confident "yes," but it wasn't the right car! And, just for good measure, I did not get the name of the town where I spent the night!!

READ IT NOW

TRAVELS IN SENEGAL, THE LAND OF PEACE AND PURPOSE

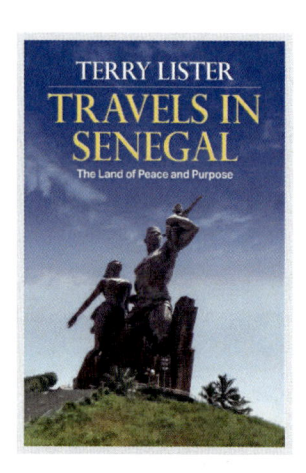

Many travellers associate Senegal with the Door of No Return—the place where over two million Africans passed through Goree Island on the way to the New World for centuries. While this is certainly a historic feature of the county, there's so much more to experience.

And world-traveller Terry Lister has proof!

Terry escorts the curious reader along Senegal's culture-rich coast as he explores national landmarks, stumbles upon unexpected African markets, and makes new friends along the way, notwithstanding debilitating language barriers. Of course, there are the familiar squabbles with border patrolmen and taxi drivers. Yet all these experiences are what make this amusing short-read both educational and unforgettable.

If you've got one hour, you've got time to travel to Senegal: The Land of Peace and Purpose.

EXCERPT

After three years in Central and South America, I was now in Africa. Senegal had been selected as the place from which I should start my African adventure, and so I left Bermuda, flew to New York on to Paris, and finally arrived in Dakar, the capital of Senegal. My long journey ended with a nighttime arrival.

The fun and games started almost immediately! I was processed by immigration without incident, obtained local currency, and retrieved my bag, but when I got outside, there was a very long taxi line. No one paid me much mind, so I had difficulty determining if I was in the right place.

Remembering the saying, "the policeman is your friend", I returned to the terminal and explained my situation to a police officer on duty. He quickly went out with me, signaled a *man over, and* told him to take me to my hotel.

Great! Can't beat that!

I followed this man a long distance away from the other taxis. I became a little concerned, but the policeman had been the one to put me in the situation, so I figured I should be all right. We headed off, and it soon became obvious that my driver had no idea where the hotel was. I did my best to explain, even showing him the route on my *maps.me* app.

Nothing helped.

Finally, I requested he call the hotel, and after a brief conversation with the staff, he said he knew where to go. I was becoming annoyed. This signaled the return of the number one problem I experienced in Central and South America—fussing with taxi drivers. We finally arrived, and it was time to pay the driver for the long-winded journey. To be prepared, before leaving Bermuda, I had checked the taxi rate and was told that the fare would be US $13. This man, who could not find the hotel, wanted US $88.

Wrong target, partner!

After what had become the usual amount of arguing, I paid him US $18.

The next day, I planned to relax and move around slowly; however, the establishment owner came to my room and told me I needed to go to the office of the cell phone company to get a sim card. He projected it would be a very busy day, and they were closing at 12 PM. Words for the wise!

I got up, quickly ate breakfast, and headed out for the cell phone company, per the owner's recommendation. He was right: long lines, plenty of confusion, and the minor fact that I didn't speak the language. Getting a sim card took forever, but eventually I got it and returned to the hotel to relax.

READ IT NOW

THE GAMBIA, THE SMILING COAST

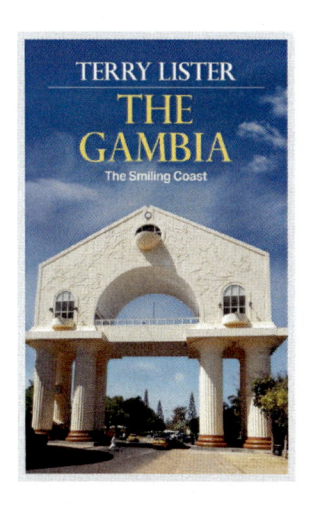

After viewing the British television show, 'Desmonds' and hearing one of the characters talk about his homeland, The Gambia, Terry Lister decided he had to visit. Equipped with this determination and a valid passport, he makes his way to the West African coast to experience the sights and wonders of this beautiful country.

Both the expected and unexpected await the prolific world traveller as he meets up with old friends and makes new ones. From encounters with leaping gorillas to brushes with evil spirits, Lister exposes the curious reader to many of the spectacles and delights of The Gambia in this hilarious and educational short-read.

If you've got one hour, you've got time to explore The Gambia: The Smiling Coast.

EXCERPT

Senegal, formerly a colony of France, has a richness that can only be understood by travelling there.

But be prepared for surprises!

The vast majority of people do not speak French. Instead, they speak the native language of *Wolof*. Thus, brushing up on your high school French will not help you get a cab most times!

The history, Gorée Island, the culture, the people—I experienced all of this in Dakar, the exceptionally vibrant capital city, during the first week of my trip. With fifteen million people, Senegal is on the rise. There is a flavour about it that fills not only your nose but your very soul.

Be open to it.

The African Renaissance Monument, the largest statue in Africa, is in Dakar. In stark contrast to the historical horrors embodied in Gorée Island, this statue stands as a tribute to the resiliency of the human spirit.

Be prepared to witness the enthusiasm of the young boys operating mule carts and their slightly older brothers operating the horses that race goods around various parts of the city.

I have been travelling through the Americas but now I am in Africa. I will experience many new things, including beautiful people who love life and refuse to be beaten down, taxi men who will take advantage if given half a chance, history that is so alive that I feel it everywhere and most of all, the chance to immerse myself in all of it. I look forward to the time that I will spend on this continent learning and living, and growing as a person as I get older. Africa, take hold of me!

Read on and experience Senegal with me!

READ IT NOW

PEACE, JOY AND LOVE: CHRISTMAS ACROSS AFRICA

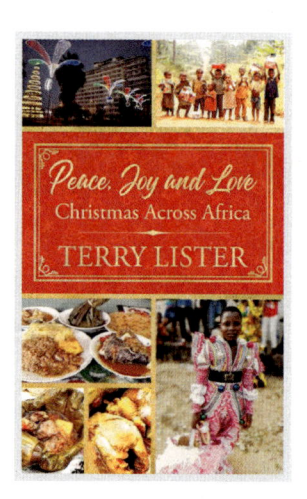

For some living in highly developed societies, Christmas is a time of exorbitant expense and sheer panic. Children are suddenly acutely aware of their conduct, and parents subconsciously feel pressured to tackle pricey wish lists.

But in Africa, Christmas is a little different, especially depending on the country you decide to visit.

Terry Lister's experiences and research gives the reader a glimpse into the customs and practices of more than 13 African nations, delivering an educational taste of the traditional foods and common rituals. Vibrant photographs display the cultural variety and demonstrate the ways in which unlikely communities work together to make the season a festive time for all, including the most impoverished.

There are lessons to be learned and adventures to be had within the pages of this literary travel treasure. Explore Christmas in Africa and prepare to walk away challenged on the concepts of what it really means to have peace, joy and love during the holiday season.

EXCERPT

In Uganda, preparation for Christmas celebration starts as early as mid-November. At this time, the radio stations start playing Christmas songs and highlighting special offers and promotions for products. These activities and other festivities will run until January 2nd. While this period is referred to as the *Christmas festive season*, the proper name for Christmas in Uganda is *Sekukulu*, and one wishes another a Merry Christmas by saying "*Sekukulu ennungi*".

At this time of the year, members of the family build up their expectations for special things like new shoes and clothes for the entire family. They also begin to focus on special family meals for Christmas day, gatherings, gift sharing and outings for the evening of December 25th. As the days draw closer to the 15th, poor husbands or men start panicking, as they need all the money they can get their hands on so they can buy a bull for slaughtering. Women also seek to put some money together, but their aim is to buy rice.

For those who are able to buy new outfits for their families, they tend to buy them a lot earlier and keep them hidden until Christmas Day. This gift buying ritual is a relatively new practice and is mainly done in the cities. Many of the people in the rural areas live in poverty, so gifts are more practical, such as meats or vegetables grown in the fields near the rivers. Children in Uganda do not believe in Santa Claus, which is why they never expect any gifts other than new clothes, should their family be able to buy them.

READ IT NOW

Made in the USA
Columbia, SC
06 July 2023